The Side School

The Side School

The story of a rural school in Renfrewshire, Scotland

1796 to 1951

David Roe

First Published 1996

© David Roe
Published by David Roe
Syde, Kilmacolm
Renfrewshire
Scotland PA13 4TG
Tel. (for re-ordering) 01505 874279

ISBN 0 9528880 0 9

Printed and bound by the Universities Print Unit
University of Strathclyde

Acknowledgements

My thanks to all those who helped in this project, and in particular the following past pupils of Side and their friends and relatives who gave their enthusiastic support: David Black, James Black, John Blair, Dr. James Browning, Robert Dunlop, Bill Kerr, Jean Hepburn, Elizabeth Hepburn, Ruby Laird, Alexander McDougall, Alastaire McIntyre, Jessie McLeod, Sheila Campbell, Isobel Orr, Robin Orr, William Ross and James Ross. Also my special thanks to Irene Dunn, archivist of the Kilmacolm Civic Trust, Sandra McDougall of the Inverclyde Library and Elizabeth Main, all of whom gave me valuable help and encouragement.

The following people kindly loaned the photographs that are reproduced in this book: *Nigel MacMillan and family* (page 21): Sheila Campbell, *School building c.1919* (page 43): Bill Kerr, *Rev. Dr. Murray* (page 48): Irene Dunn, *Horatio Peile* (page 48): John Wilson, *Rev. Thos. Gregory* (page 49): Irene Dunn, *Rev James Fyfe* (page 49): Irene Dunn, *School Photograph 1894* (page79): Jessie McLeod, *Queen Victoria's Jubilee celebrations in Kilmacolm* (page 84): Irene Dunn, *Donald McDonald and William Walker* (page 87): Irene Dunn, *School photograph c1900* (page 88): Isobel Orr, *School photograph c.1905* (page 94): James Ross, *Robert Orr at Gateside Farm* (page 102): Ruby Laird, *School photograph c.1919* (page 108): Elizabeth and Jean Hepburn, *School photograph c.1924* (page 110): James Black, *School photograph 1951* (page 121): Irene Dunn and James Browning.

Contents

Preface		9
1: The Old Subscription School	c1796 to 1863	11
2: Side People		17
3: The Dominie		27
4: The New Subscription School	1863 to 1874	31
5: Side becomes a Public School	1874	39
6: The School Board		45
7: William Campbell	1873 to 1877	53
8: Stewart Archibald	1877 to 1884	61
9: Annie Craig Bell	1884 to 1905	73
10: Mabel Maclaren	1905 to 1930	91
11: Elizabeth Browning	1930 to 1951	115
Epilogue		123
Bibliography		126
The Teachers		127
The School Managers		128

The Side School

Preface

About two hundred years ago, probably in about 1796, a small farming community in the parish of Kilmacolm in Western Scotland decided to give their children a regular education. It was not a casual decision to send their children down the road to school: there wasn't one. It was a major community project to obtain a plot of land, build a school on it and hire a teacher. The community was not particularly wealthy, and they must have had a firm belief in the value of education to take on such a major project, knowing that they would get no help from either the state or the parish.

The school they built was typical of buildings of that time and place, a primitive affair with a roof of turf and an earth floor. It had just two apartments: one for the teacher to live in, the other for the classroom. Nevertheless it lasted for 70 years, at which time the community, wanting better facilities for their children, erected a superior building, which with extensions and improvements made over the years still stands today.

When starting to research the history of the school, I was taken by surprise by the wealth of information available, which tells the story, not just of bricks and mortar, but of the lives of the community around the school. The story takes us through the dramatic social changes of one and a half centuries, through the reigns of seven monarchs, two World Wars, the General Strike and the Depression, all of which touched the lives of the children and their parents. It takes us from the time when providing an education for one's children was a highly prized objective to be fought for at private expense, to the time when education became compulsory for all children, when parents discovered that they no longer had the option of keeping their children from school to help out on the farm at busy times.

First hand accounts dating from the 1850's give detailed descriptions both of the school itself and the lives of the children and their teachers. They tell how the children were taught, how they worked and how they played, and of the work and social life of the parish. Starting in 1875 when the school was transferred into the public education system, we get the teachers record of events in the school log book, in which the teacher wrote his or her account of the main activities of the week. Equally informative are the minutes of the School Board of the parish, through which we can follow the efforts of the board to implement the provisions of the Education Act of 1872 which made education compulsory for all children. The School Board did not confine themselves to educational matters, but got involved with the moral, religious and medical welfare of the children. These original documents make fascinating reading and are available for study in the Glasgow City Archives.

For the 1920's onwards, I was able to obtain first hand accounts from a number of ex-pupils who attended the school at that time. Some of them returned to the classroom for the first time since they left the school some seventy years earlier to tell their stories, the environment of the old building helping them recall the memories of their school days.

Chapter One
The Old Subscription School
c1796 to 1863

George III was on the throne when they built the first school at Side, already experiencing the bouts of insanity that later lead to his confinement and to his son the Prince of Wales becoming Regent.

The last half century had been eventful. Fifty years earlier while the King's grandson, George II was on the throne, the last engagement of the Jacobite uprising had taken place at Culloden. Twenty years earlier a colony had been lost when America gained her independence, while on the other side of the world a new colony was being settled, though no one yet knew whether the Australian continent consisted of one island or several. The French Revolution had just about run its course and France had declared war with Britain. The battles of Trafalgar and Waterloo were less than twenty years in the future.

Nearer to home, Robert Burns was in the last months of his life, having given up farming as well as his life as a celebrity - the "ploughman poet" - in the capital, in favour of a career as an excise man. And all the while the industrial revolution was in progress. Scores of factories had been built powered by the new improved steam engines developed by James Watt, born in Greenock, five miles from the Side school. The steam-

1: The Old Subscription School: c1796 to 1863

ship Charlotte Dundas was about to complete her successful trials on the Clyde, and the steam locomotive was soon to make its first journey

Meanwhile, in the rather remote parish of Kilmacolm, the Industrial Revolution had so far not touched the lives of the community, when a few children, perhaps 20 or 30, entered their classroom for the first time to begin their education in Reading, Writing, Arithmetic and the Scriptures.

We get the first detailed description of Side from a newspaper article written by James Slater in 1856 entitled *"A Run Through Kilmacolm"*:

Tuesday, June 24, 1856. — **The Greenock Advertiser and Clyde Commercial Journal**

"On the braeface near Gateside stands a lonely and lowly building, the schoolhouse of the district. It was built about 60 years ago by public subscription, and its accommodation consists of the school room, about 12 feet square, and a "but and ben" (two roomed cottage) for the teacher. The whole appearance of the house, both out and in, is of the most primitive description - earthen floors and turf roofs- and, if we remember right, an old worn-out millstone, placed in the centre of the school floor, served at once for grate and hearth, for which a liberal supply of peats is provided against the winter. Peats are the chief fuel with all the inhabitants of this locality. Each farmer in the barony is allowed to go into the moor and cast as many peats as will serve him for fuel during the winter. When we visited this school many years ago, we found the present teacher labouring away with some twenty or thirty pupils, several of whom were under the inspection of the Parochial board of Greenock, and boarded with some of the families in the neighbourhood. The attainments of the scholars, especially in arithmetic, were creditable to the industry and attention of their master, who has contrived to eke out an existence in this lonesome place, for the best part of twenty years"

The Side School

James Slater was a teacher at Glenmill, a school on the other side of the Side hill two or three miles from the Side school.

It cannot have been easy to teach - or to learn - in those conditions. Imagine a smoke filled room only twelve feet square into which are packed up to thirty children and the master, not to mention the millstone with the fire grate on top. There would not have been space for desks, and the children would have been sitting either on the ground, or at best on wooden benches- not the ideal circumstances for learning to write. Nor would the bible be the ideal book for learning to read. One wonders why Greenock folk would send their children to this remote school with its primitive facilities when there would surely have been superior alternatives in the town of Greenock itself. Perhaps the school or teacher had an unusually high reputation that had reached the town, or maybe they thought that there would be fewer distractions for their children in the countryside.

From James Slater's account we can deduce that the old school was built in about 1796[1]. At this time of course education was not compulsory, nor was it freely provided by the state. There was an obligation on the heritors to provide a school in each parish, and by the time the Side school was built there was already a parish school in the village of Kilmacolm, having an attendance of about 40 children in the summer and 30 in the winter. But because the population was mostly of farming families and farm workers dispersed throughout the parish, there were many children who could not get to the village school. For this reason a number of small schools were established, scattered throughout the parish, in contrast to present day arrangements with larger more centralised schools. In the early eighteen hundreds, six schools were recorded, typically only two or three miles apart. There was the parish school and subscription schools at Side, Glenmill and Pennytersal, each of which was funded by its local community. The other two were probably adventure schools, run for profit. Adventure schools tended to vary in quality from being reputable establishments to little more than child minding arrangements. Some children may also have been educated through the practice where the teacher did not have a permanent school building, but went

---

[1]*The exact date of building the old school is unknown. Other than James Slater's estimate, the earliest reference to Side is in the parish records of 1816.*

from farm to farm, lodging at each for a time and teaching the children in the immediate neighbourhood before moving on. This was the manner in which Robert Burns received his early education.

James Slater's article was not the first reference to Side. In the early years of the school there are occasional references in the minutes of the heritors (land owners) of the parish, usually in the form of requests from the residents near Side for financial assistance in running the school. But the heritors were more concerned with the parish school in the village for which they were responsible, and which was financed by the taxes they paid.

The earliest known teachers in the parish were listed in the church records of 1800 as Thomas MacMillan, Charles Gordon and Thomas Cummins. Thomas MacMillan was the teacher in the village school, so one of the other two was probably the teacher at Side, though which of the two is not known.

In 1816, the parish records record the baptism of a son to *"Robert Muir, teacher in Westside and Marry McKee his spouse"*. They had three more children, in 1817, 1819 and 1822. The records show that by the time their third child was born in 1819 they had moved to Glenside, presumably the school near Glenmill. If we are to believe James Slater's description, they would have been pleased to give up the struggle of raising a family in the primitive schoolhouse at Side in favour of the superior accommodation at Glenmill. In Slater's words:

> *"There is another district school in the south side of the parish near Glenmill, most romantically situated on the bank of a fine rivulet. The accommodation here is in every way superior, and we could name several teachers who have risen to eminence in their profession who first commenced to wield the ferula in this little school"*

As the teacher at Glenmill, it would be reasonable to think that James Slater might be a little prejudiced.

The Side school was situated in the West of Scotland in the parish of Kilmacolm and the county of Renfrewshire, a few miles south of the River Clyde. The school described by James Slater was not the present building, which is on the turnpike -the High Greenock Road- but its predecessor, set back about 70 yards up the brae-

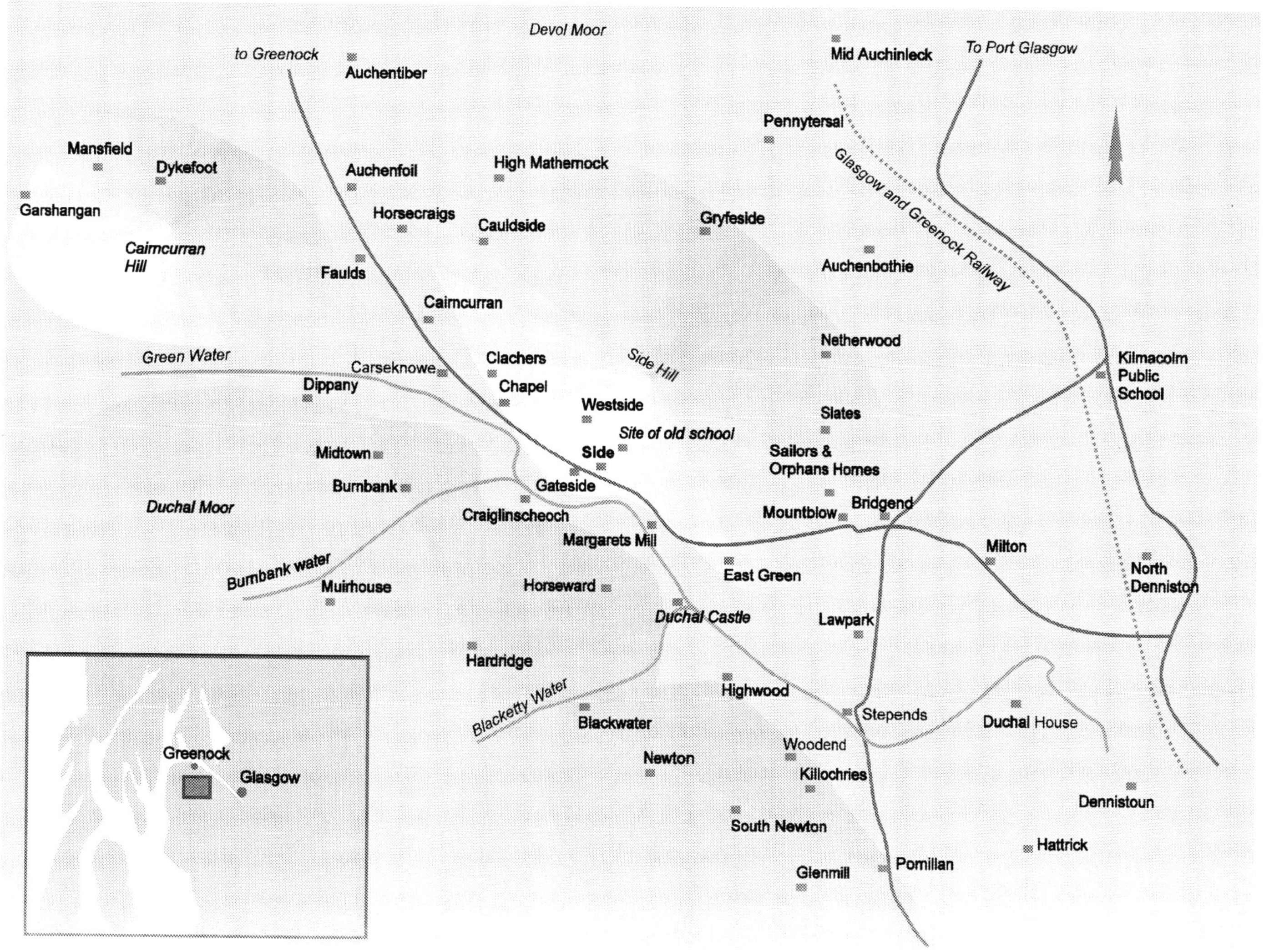
Devol Moor
to Greenock
Auchentiber
Mid Auchinleck
To Port Glasgow
Pennytersal
Mansfield
Dykefoot
Auchenfoil
High Mathernock
Garshangan
Horsecraigs
Cauldside
Gryfeside
Glasgow and Greenock Railway
Cairncurran Hill
Faulds
Auchenbothie
Cairncurran
Netherwood
Green Water
Carseknowe
Clachers
Side Hill
Kilmacolm Public School
Dippany
Chapel
Westside
Slates
Site of old school
Midtown
Side
Sailors & Orphans Homes
Burnbank
Gateside
Duchal Moor
Craiglinscheoch
Mountblow
Bridgend
Margarets Mill
Milton
Burnbank water
East Green
North Denniston
Muirhouse
Horseward
Duchal Castle
Lawpark
Hardridge
Highwood
Blacketty Water
Stepends
Duchal House
Blackwater
Greenock
Woodend
Newton
Glasgow
Killochries
Dennistoun
South Newton
Hattrick
Pomillan
Glenmill

side. Along the turnpike farmers drove their cattle and delivered their produce of potatoes, meal and milk to the town of Greenock 5 miles away, a two hour journey by milk cart. The turnpike was a narrow rutted track, with passing places to allow carts to pass. It followed the valley of the Green Water between the Side Hill to the East and Duchal Moor to the West, before climbing the hills on the outskirts of Greenock to reveal magnificent views over the valley of the river Clyde.

Two hundred years later the journey to Greenock takes only 15 minutes, but the landscape has hardly changed. The hills with rocky outcrops and small fields bounded by stone dykes are now used only to graze sheep and cattle. The farm buildings are built of stone with roofs of slate which 200 years ago would have been mostly turf. There are few trees. It is an attractive, craggy kind of landscape, not magnificent or awe-inspiring- the hills are only a few hundred feet high - but a million miles from the prettier pastoral region of the South. There are no extremes of temperature, and the snowfall is usually modest, but it can be a bleak place in winter with frequent gales and driving rain. Though it is only two miles from Side to the village of Kilmacolm with its parish school, it was too far for young children to travel each day because of the primitive roads and the severe winter weather, and it was the younger children who got most of the education, the older children having to work on the farm when they were strong enough.

The low hill known as the Side hill gives its name to the school as well as to many nearby farms such as *Gateside, West Side, Burnside and Cauldside*. Throughout its history the school was variously known as the Side School, the Syde School, or West Side School. Confusingly, a "side" school was a description commonly given to an additional school founded by the heritors in a very large parish for children who lived too far to be able to travel to the main school. In some respects this description applies to Side, but technically Side was a subscription school, funded by the local community, and not a side school which was funded by local taxes.

# Chapter Two
Side People

Today, within a mile of Side there are some twenty farm buildings, though in only a handful of them is farming the principal business. In the first part of the nineteenth century there were almost twice as many farms[1], and in practically all of them farming provided the livelihood of the occupants. Not only was the density of farm buildings greater, but so was the number of people in each farm. Some farms supported two or more independent farming families, each having their own farm servants. For example, the census of 1841 showed that Auchenfoil was farmed by Hugh and Ann Blair, their three children, a female servant and a disabled seaman, together with Donald and Janet Black and their children Hugh and Rachael. At that time Donald Black was a farm labourer, but 50 years later at the age of 76 he farmed there in his own right, and more than 100 years later still his descendants continue to farm there. Later on he became a member of the management committee for the Side school.

---

[1] *Some of the farms and farm cottages that have disappeared over the years or are in ruins are: West Green, East Side, Mutehill, Wardwell, Horseward, Midtown, High Craiglinscheoch, High Heugh, Laigh Heugh, High Woodhead and Laigh Woodhead.*

Census records of the mid eighteen hundreds show that farm servants were employed as ploughmen, shepherds, dairymaids, nursery maids, farm labourers and house servants. In addition a number of paupers on parish relief were boarded out at farms in the area. At Clachers Cottage, Ann McGill boarded 6 children between the ages of 5 and 10, each described as a pauper and a scholar, their education being presumably at Side at the expense of the parish. This arrangement may well have been a better alternative for the children than the poorhouse, depending on how well they were treated by their foster parents.

Some of the households were employed in more specialist work. Between 1841 and 1891 families at Mountblow supported the community in trades such as blacksmith, joiner, master wright, cooper and dike builder, with younger men in the household learning their crafts as apprentices. In 1841 at Gateside farm, just across the road from Side, Mrs. Janet Hunter declared her occupation as innkeeper. Thirty years later there were three families living at Gateside, two of them engaged in farming and the other in weaving, one of a handful of families who had strayed from the more traditional weaving areas in the county. Highwood cottage was for some years occupied by a gamekeeper and his family.

Muirhouse, a farm about a mile from the school on Duchal moor, is of particular interest as the home of Nigel MacMillan, a scholar at the old school who left us with vivid descriptions of life in the middle of the 19th century, and in particular his recollections of the school. His school days in the eighteen fifties left a lasting impression on him, and when he retired from farming at the age of eighty, he gave a lecture entitled *"Memories of Old Times: Changes in Customs and Habits"* to the Dumfries Natural History and Antiquarian Society, reminiscing about his childhood days. This is what he said about his old school:

"the side school, an old thatched biggin' consisting of two apartments with a coal bunker between. In one end the Master, a bachelor lived; the school in the other. The floor was of clay, with a smooth topped flat whinstone in the centre; upon this stood the fire grate, a circular iron cage about two feet high. It was not a fixture; in dull weather the smoke, instead of ascending through an opening about 6 feet square directly above the fire, filled the school room with dense pungent reek. The fire had

then to be carried outside until the smoke abated, when it was carried back to its place. The opening, six feet square above the fire communicated with a loft the whole length of the building. When the loft was filled with reek it made its way out by the lum head.

Few books were used besides the Bible and Shorter catechism or "Questions" as we called the hated task book. Long stretches of the bible were read verse about, finishing off the day with singing Psalm tunes. "Kilmarnock", "Coleshill", and "Evan" were the favourites".

He obviously had an excellent memory, his description of the school corresponding closely with James Slater's contemporary account. The Natural History and Antiquarian Society must have had an enjoyable evening as Mr. MacMillan entertained them with a colourful account of the days of his youth. He talked about his school friends Jock Love and Jamie Dunlop and their courting experiences, about the primitive medical practices of the time- his father had qualified as a doctor before he took up farming- and about the busy period on Sundays in the village's three grog shops when the congregation took refreshment between morning and afternoon sermons.

Nigel MacMillan's grandfather was a Highlander who had settled in Greenock, making such a good living there as a shoemaker that he was able to buy the farm at Muirhouse (a 109 acre farm for which he paid £1100) and pay for his son's (Nigel's father's) education in Glasgow where he qualified as a doctor. Dr. MacMillan practised medicine for a short time in Glasgow, but on the death of his father decided to stay at Muirhouse and try his hand at farming. Some years later he became involved in a bitter legal dispute with Sir Michael Shaw-Stewart when Sir Michael challenged his right to the ownership of Muirhouse farm. According to Nigel MacMillan's account the MacMillans won the subsequent court case, but Sir Michael had his way in the end because the MacMillans had to sell the farm to Sir Michael in order to pay their legal costs of defending the case amounting to £500, and the MacMillans ended up as Sir Michael's tenants. Nigel never forgot his father's misfortune as his bitter recollections written 35 years after the event show. Nigel left the parish of Kilmacolm at the age of 25 and farmed for a while near Largs before moving to Kirkconnel in Nithsdale, Dumfriesshire.

During his long career in farming, Nigel found that although the occupation demanded all of his physical energy, his mind was free to dwell on more philosophical matters. Being something of a poet, he found time to write a few lines about the events that interested him, covering matters as diverse as family bereavements, the conduct of the Boer War and the appearance of Halley's comet. A few examples of his work are quoted later in this book.

In his retirement lecture to the Dumfries Natural History and Antiquarian Society, he went on to give a graphic account of other activities at the school. Evidently it was something of a social centre as well as being a place of education:

> *"Work had the first call upon those who were able to do something to help on the farm. In busy seasons boys and girls 11 to 15 years of age would lend their assistance. But to make up for this, during the winter months a night school for the big boys and girls was run from October till the end of March. Young men and maidens, some of them well through their teens, attended regularly. There was a dance following lessons on one or two nights each week. One of the big boys would approach the Dominie with a request for a dance, which the good old soul freely granted. Then the fun began. "Steek (shut) the door and keep in the women" shouted Jock Love. The small boys and girls went home; the others went at the dance with a will. For music one of the party "deedled", beating time with a pair of tongs. The master of ceremonies shouted orders above the din to awkward boys at critical moments, such as "Grup your woman, Jock"; reel hooch. Above the din was heard the rhythmic beat of the tongs accompanied by musical lilting of merry tunes to suit the dance. In these days of Fox-trots and Tangos it is refreshing to look back at the homely ways of our ancestors."*

The *"days of Fox-trots and Tangos"* that Mr. MacMillan referred to were the days of 1926 when he gave his lecture. He went on to describe what happened on the Sabbath, when people came from neighbouring parishes to the Kirk in Kilmacolm, walking long distances barefoot over the hills from as far afield as Largs. As they approached the village they put on their shoes that had been carried with them, not wishing to appear in church with muddy shoes.

---

right: Nigel MacMillan and his family

The Side School

These were the days of long sermons and services in both the morning and afternoon. Between sermons they had an hour to prepare themselves for the afternoon session, and some of them made use of the facilities of the grog shops in the village. There was a choice of three: the Black Bull, the Saint Malcolm, and the Lairds Inn. In July 1856 several of the householders in the village petitioned the heritors, complaining about the *"want of a police force"* and referring to the *"disgraceful scenes last Sabbath"*. Evidently some of the folk had overdone their preparation for the afternoon sermon. The petitioners asked that a policeman from Greenock should be transferred to Kilmacolm, but since the total police force in Greenock at this time amounted to just two men, it is unlikely that their request was taken very seriously.

It was in church that lads and lassies would most often find an opportunity to become acquainted, but as Nigel MacMillan explained, protocol demanded a proper introduction:

"A young man at kirk or fair had fancied some fair maid, but had not the privilege of her acquaintance. But he knew that his chum Jock Love was on friendly terms with her people and he would see if Jock would gie him a "black fit". "Ou aye: I'll dae that Jamie, and faur mair for ye. What dae ye say to the nicht o' the Glasgow Stallion Show?" "Aw richt, Jock, I'll meet ye at the show" In the gloaming of a chilly spring day in the early sixties of last century I was one of four who presented ourselves at a well-known farm between Port Glasgow and Kilmacolm. I was curious to know what was meant by "black fit". Jock Love who was well acquainted with the three pretty daughters went forward to the door along with his chum, Jamie, who stood back about a couple of yards while Jock knocked. One of the girls answered. "Oh, it's you Jock. Come awa ben." "Wheesht," said Jock, "would ye tell yer sister Maggie that I hae a lad here that would like unco weel tae see her. He's a rale decent chiel." The girl returned to the kitchen and told her sister how the land lay. Maggie at once came to the door, shook hands with Jock, who introduced her to his chum, Jamie, in the dark. The mystery was solved - simply an introduction in the dark to the girl that he desired to meet. We were all invited to come awa in where we spent a couple of happy hours. Those courting romances lightened and brightened the young farmer's life and provided no end of talk for

The Side School

the lads and the lassies"

Jock Love was obviously a bit of a lad, a key figure in evening dancing after lessons and a *"black fit"* - a lovers go between - in courting activities. He was a couple of years older than Nigel MacMillan and the son of Alexander and Agnes Love of Margarets Mill.

The mill drew its power from the Green water a couple of hundred yards from Side and was one of three mills that served the needs of the parish. The mill is now a ruin but the farm continues to exist. The Love family who lived there for the whole of the nineteenth and much of the twentieth centuries crop up from time to time in the history of the school. Alexander and Agnes Love (described as *"millar and farmer's wife"* in the census records) had eight children, Jock being the seventh. Alexander the oldest son took over at Margarets Mill when his father died, and Jock and his brother Robert set up as farmers first at Gateside then at West Side. In spite of his romantic excursions, Jock never married.

But who was Maggie and who were the three pretty sisters who received a visit from Nigel MacMillan, Jock Love and Jamie in the early sixties at the *"well known farm between Port Glasgow and Kilmacolm"*? At this time, in say 1863, Nigel and Jock were 18 and 20 years old respectively. The most likely candidates for the objects of their attention appear to be the children of Mr. Arthur Lang and his wife Christian who farmed at Mid Auchinleck on the Port Glasgow Road, now swallowed up by a housing estate on the outskirts of Port Glasgow. The census of 1861 shows that the Langs had seven children, including three teenage daughters: Agnes, Margaret and Christian, who would have been 18, 17 and 15 years old respectively in 1863.

Just how the relationship between Maggie and Jamie developed is not known, but it did not lead to their marriage. A few years afterwards, Agnes married an engineer from Greenock, Maggie married a man from a neighbouring farm at Bardrainney, and Christina married a clerk from Greenock.

***

It is tempting to imagine that before the railway came people never, or at any rate rarely, travelled outside the boundaries of the parish. But there were exceptions to this conventional picture of rural life. Nigel MacMillan for one left the county to live initially at Largs and eventually near Dumfries. He also tells us about a cousin of his who travelled much further afield:

"My cousin Agnes MacMillan of Greenock, now Mrs. Bancroft of 128 Hambledon, Melbourne Australia, was in my boyish days 50 years ago a frequent visitor at Muirhouse Kilmacolm. A wild impetuous girl full of fun and frolic. Alas! the worlds thorny ways all too soon envolved(?) her round. She married early a sea captain who died. Again she ventured upon marriage, this time Mr. Bancroft a gentleman of good position in Melbourne. He lost his money and died, leaving his widow ill provided for and age creeping upon her, age and want. She frequently turned her thoughts to the wild happy romping days of her youth far away in Bonnie Scotland".

***

People's attitude towards education in the early eighteenth century was varied, as shown by some of the proverbial quotations that have been passed down to us. For example:

" a boy's education is completed when he has been four or five winters at school: after that he has only to work, no more time needs to be spent on mental improvement"

It may be that this tradition was based more on the desire to make use of the child's ability to do useful work on the farm after the age of 10 or 11 than on his or her educational needs. One old sage of the time said he:

"had never read a yard o' print since he left the school and yet he ken'd full as muckle about horse an kye beasts as the minister and had a hunner pounds in the bank".

The reality was that by 1836 everyone in the parish could read, if we are to believe the account of the minister, Robert Cameron, writing about the parish of Kilmacolm in the New Statistical Account of Scotland in 1836:

"There are no persons in the parish who cannot read, and the young do so remarkably well. All seem alive to the benefits and necessity of education".

This is in accord with the tradition that the provision of education for all children in Scotland was established sooner than in England. Daniel Defoe, writing in the early eighteenth century said:

The Side School

> *"You will find very few (Scottish) gentry either ignorant or unlearned. Nay you cannot ordinarily find a servant in Scotland but he can read or write".*

The local farming community were clearly *"alive to the benefit and necessity of education"*. They could ill-afford to have their children take time off from farm work, not to mention the cost of establishing a school and paying for a teacher for an activity that could scarcely be thought of great value in improving a man's - or woman's - ability to tackle the heavy physical work demanded by the farming methods of the day.

2: Side people

Chapter Three
The Dominie

The teacher they hired, *the dominie*, was invariably a man at the beginning of the nineteenth century. It was not until Victorian times that childrens' education was entrusted to a school mistress.

The dominie was a respected member of the community, but the job was poorly paid, though nowhere nearly as poorly paid as is often suggested in accounts of the time. In 1843 the teacher in the parish school in Kilmacolm was James Blackburn. He got an annual salary of £34-4-4 (£34.22) as well as his accommodation in the schoolhouse. In addition to his salary he was paid an allowance of £2-2-8 (£2.13) because the school house did not have a garden. By way of comparison, in the same period a farm worker in Renfrewshire earned about £25 per annum, and an Ayrshire weaver £15 to £18 per annum. This was not the whole of James Blackburn's income however. During the course of his career he made use of his abilities as an educated man by taking on a number of other jobs in the village. By the time he retired in 1854 he was established in the offices of Parish Registrar of Births Marriages and Deaths, Collector and Clerk to the Heritors, Collector and Clerk to the Road Trustees, and Session Clerk. As collector to the heritors he was responsible for collecting taxes from the heritors in proportion to their property valuations and redistributing the money to tradesmen working on public works in the parish such as building work on the church, the manse and the village school. He often had to perform quite a difficult balancing act between the demands of tradesman wanting to be paid for their work, and collecting money from heritors who were not in the habit of paying up at the first or even second time of asking. However these offices made a welcome contribution of about £10 each to his income. When he retired he got a lifetime pension equal to his full salary as a teacher plus an allowance of £5 for rent, since he gave up the occupancy of the schoolhouse on retirement. In total, the income from his salary as teacher, his allowances, pension and income from other positions, together with his accommodation at the school house gave him quite a reasonable living by the standards of the time.

The same was not true of the other teachers in the parish, such as Daniel Ferguson, the Side dominie between about 1836 and 1864 who taught Nigel MacMillan and Jock Love. His income came mainly from school fees, this arrangement encouraging him to use all his influence to promote school attendance. He only got about £15 or £20 a year, together with his primitive accommodation in the school building. There was little opportunity to take on additional work as there was for James Blackburn in the village. He might have been able to grow a few vegetables or keep a few chickens in the little plot of land next to the school. He was a bachelor, not surprisingly perhaps: the single-apartment school house was not designed for a married couple with a family.

The fact that local taxes were used to pay the costs of running the village school and the village teacher's salary, but not the Side teacher's salary, was a sore point with the parents of Side school children. They were paying for both the village school and the school that their children attended. In 1857 when the village school was rebuilt the assessment on some of the residents near Side for the rebuilding work was:

James Anderson Jnr. of Blacksholm	£29 -18 -11
Alexander Love of Margarets Mill	£3 -19 - 2
Robert Blair of Pomillan	£2 - 3 - 6
Robert Lang of Gateside	£13 -14 - 2
Alexander Crawford of Chapel	£3 - 9 - 3

The Side parents petitioned the heritors *"craving aid to*

The Side School

the teacher of the Side School", but the Education Act then in force did not allow any payment collected for the parish teacher to be paid to anyone else. However the heritors found a way round this piece of bureaucracy by having the parish teacher agree to pay £2 out of his salary to each of the teachers at Glenmill, Side and Pennytersal. They petitioned again in 1861, and this time the village teacher was to pay the Side teacher on a sliding scale depending on his own salary, which effectively increased his contribution to £5.

When a teaching position became vacant, the school managers would advertise for a new teacher from the pulpit and in the Greenock, Glasgow and Edinburgh newspapers. The parish teacher was expected to be capable of teaching Reading, Writing, Arithmetic, Decimals, Latin, Greek and Book-keeping. If he could also teach Navigation that was regarded as a bonus, and it was taken for granted that he would also teach the Scriptures. Navigation and Book-keeping were subjects offered to provide career choices to the children in addition to farming, and Latin was taught because it was a pre-requisite to university entrance. However at the Side school there was no call for such exotic subjects and the teacher was not expected to tackle more than Reading, Writing, Arithmetic and of course the Scriptures.

There was no shortage of applicants for vacancies, and when James Blackburn retired from the village school in 1854 there were 62 applicants for the post. Eleven were short listed and interviewed. Donald MacDonald, the successful candidate, was given written confirmation of his selection by the heritors. He then had to present himself at the presbytery in Paisley to have his appointment formally confirmed. The church still exercised considerable authority in educational matters, as they did of course on all aspects of life.

Chapter Four
The New Subscription School
1863 to 1874

The Parish of Kilmacolm went through a turning point in the 1850s. The population of this remote farming community - *"out of the world and into Kilmacolm"* they used to say- decreased from 1616 in 1841 to 1399 in 1851. The chief reason for the decrease according to the 1851 census was that many of the farms had changed from arable to livestock, thereby reducing the need for employing farm labourers. When James Slater wrote his newspaper article about Kilmacolm in 1856, he suggested that *"if depopulation goes on for the next thirty years as it has for the last, it will indeed be a deserted village".*

But the new advances of the Victorian age were coming to Kilmacolm and the village was to take on a new role. Queen Victoria herself visited Greenock on August 17, 1847 on her way to a tour of the West Highlands with her husband. Her diary tells us that as many as 39 steamers crowded with sightseers followed the royal yacht and many more watched from the shore. Maybe some of the Side children hitched a ride on the milk cart to Greenock to see the royal party.

The railway came and the station at Kilmacolm opened in 1869, connecting the village to nearby towns of Greenock and Paisley and the city of Glasgow. Modern conveniences such as gas lighting came in 1873 and a piped water supply in 1878. Within a few decades the village was transformed. Smart new houses were built for wealthy commuters who worked in Glasgow and Paisley and lived in the increasingly fashionable village of Kilmacolm. The village became a popular destination for weekend excursions for the workers in the surrounding towns of Paisley, Port Glasgow and Greenock as described in the report in the Paisley and Renfrew Gazette in April 1873:

April 26, 1873   ***Paisley and Renfrew Gazette***

KILMACOLM
THE MARCH OF IMPROVEMENT- Since the opening of the Ayrshire Railway, Kilmacolm has undergone a complete transformation. As an old "out-o'-the-way" Scottish clachan of one-storey thatched houses, with its kirk and public house on opposite sides of the road, within a few yards of each other, and its schule and smiddy, there is hardly an old house left. They have been pulled down and handsome two storey modern houses erected in their stead. In the course of last year twenty new houses at least were built, intended to be let as residences during the summer months - the purity of the atmosphere without the keenness of the air at seaside residences being considered particularly favourable for bronchial complaints. The Buchanan Arms, a hotel in the modern style, has been erected- a really comfortable house- where accommodation fit for a prince may be had and charges not unreasonable. Here families come from Glasgow, Paisley, Greenock &etc. to stay for a week or two for the benefit of a change of air and find themselves just as cheap as if they had gone into lodgings. Mrs. Laird of the old Kilmacolm Inn still survives the march of progress. She is eighty five years of age and takes charge of her Old Hostelrie- famous in its day for ham and egg breakfasts and dinners and where yet good entertainment after the

old style can be had, and which is largely patronised. The post mistress is another old and respected resident, but she cannot stand her ground. She is to be swept away in the rage for improvement. 'Tis three years since the railway was opened; but will be believed, it has never been taken advantage of for the conveyance of letters. And there has been all that time only one despatch in the 24 hours, the mail going by Port Glasgow. A letter posted at 10 am on one day would be delivered at 10 am at the same hour on the next day in Greenock or Glasgow- to either of which places it could be taken by railway in half an hour.

This anomaly exists at the present moment. It is a sad drawback to Kilmacolm. But it is to be "reformed" on Whitsunday. The Post Office is to be pulled down, the post mistress is to be replaced by a younger and more active official, there is to be a money order office and a telegraph office conjoined, and several despatches and deliveries in the course of a day. This is as it should be and will be well if the old post mistress gets a pension. Of course a rising community could not do without a bank. A branch of the Royal Bank of Scotland has been opened under the management of a Mr. Walter Holmes whose business no doubt will grow with the growth of the community. At the commencement of the agency only 12 months ago the bank was only opened twice in the week. Now it is found essential to have it opened every day. No newspaper is yet published in Kilmacolm, but there is a news agency conducted by Mr. Ferguson, chemist. And in addition to the light of literature the town is about to be supplied with gas light, a very compact gaswork having been erected which when the pipes are laid will have cost £2000 raised by a joint stock company on the limited liability principal. A water company should be formed on the same principal for the supply of pure and wholesome water from the hills above the town in the east and where a natural dam or reservoir is already provided; and the water pipes and gas pipes could be laid at the same time. Just now water is contained from a well in a hollow at the back of the New Hotel. On medical authority the water is bad. It savours of sewage and no wonder for all the surface drains into this hollow. Any place people go for health should be most particular in respect of purity of water, next in importance to the purity of its air. - Glasgow Herald

4: The New Subscription School

Back in the 1860s the community at Side could not have failed to be affected by the air of change as the navigators blasted away the rock in preparation for the railway line. By this time the old school building was about seventy years old, and regarded as primitive, even when judged by the standards of the time. Matthew Gemmel, a teacher at Bridge of Weir described the school in the *Paisley and Renfrewshire Gazette* as:

"an auld storm-battered biggin, lowly and primitive enough in its look but useful in its time".

The community again demonstrated their belief in the importance of educating their children and decided the time had come to build a new school. They would replace the *"auld biggin"* with a modern state of the art building, comparable with the new village school that had opened in 1858.

Their new school at Side was completed in 1863, a few years before the railway station opened. Dominie Daniel Ferguson at the age of 65 would have been nearing the end of his career when after about 30 years of his lonely bachelor existence in the primitive thatched schoolhouse he walked the seventy yards down the hill to move into his new and more comfortable home and start work in the new school.

The management committee responsible for the rebuilding program at Side were mostly local farmers: James Baxter of High Craiglinscheoch, Donald Black of Auchenfoil, James Chalmers, Alexander McDougall of Dippany, and John Scott, lead by their chairman, the Reverend James Eckford Fyfe.

The Reverend James Fyfe was an influential figure in the parish and was to retain an interest in the school until his death in 1898. He was the first minister of the United Presbyterian church in Kilmacolm which was founded in 1862. Nigel MacMillan described how this church was founded from the congregation that had left the Parish church en masse because they were dissatisfied with the new minister, who had been installed against their wishes under the system of patronage which then prevailed.

As with the original school, it was built without assistance from the state or the parish. The management committee chose a new site just a few yards down the hill from the old school, by the side of the Kilmacolm to Greenock turnpike. The stones from the old school were hauled down the hill to be used in the new

The Side School

building, leaving only a few foundation stones to mark the site as they continue to do over a century later. Like the old school, the land was rented from one James Anderson, a banker and landowner whose family lived at Blacksholm near Side and later at Higholm in Port Glasgow. The rent of 5 shillings (25p) per annum was never paid or requested, so Mr. Anderson effectively gifted the land.

The new building was altogether more substantial than the one it replaced, built to last like the surrounding farms, and forming the nucleus of the building that exists today. It had a slate roof in common with the new houses in the village that were replacing the old thatched buildings, and walls up to two and a half feet (750 mm) thick. The school room was about 26 feet by 18 feet (8m by 5.5m), three times the area of the old one, and lighter and airier with a 13 foot (4m) high ceiling, roof lights and generous windows, with high cills that shielded the children from outside distractions. Across the end of the school room building, forming a "T" shape, was the teacher's two-apartment house, complete with a small garden. There was a timber floor throughout, the school room and the living rooms had fireplaces with chimneys, and there were proper desks for the children.

Of course a state of the art school in 1863 lacked a few of the things we take for granted today. For example, the lighting consisted of oil lamps hanging from the ceiling, there was no running water, and there were no toilets for the children of any description.

This was of course in keeping with the much simpler lives that people lead then, when there was no piped mains water supply and only the most primitive kinds of toilet facilities. The Kilmacolm heritors' minutes of 1866 tell of a proposal to install a WC and a bath in the Manse at a cost of £39-12-2 (£39.60). The heritors were unwilling to pay for such an expensive luxury and decided to delay a decision until the next meeting, in the meantime asking the minister, the Rev Alexander Leck, to consider whether an earth closet would not be preferable. The Rev Leck persisted and eventually got his bath and WC.

Nigel MacMillan tells us of farmers and farm workers dining at the same table on broth and potatoes, varied occasionally by salted herrings that were eaten with the fingers, without the aid of knives and forks. Though their diet was simple, it was a good deal less monotonous than in poorer parts of the country where potatoes three times a day was the norm, and a good deal more nutritious than that of the poor people of the big cities. In all the school photographs the children look healthy, with none of the symptoms of rickets that are seen in similar photographs of city children. In Kilmacolm porridge, milk, oat cakes and cheese were commonly available.

Medical practices were still primitive. Although anaesthetics were starting to be used in dentistry and surgery, it was still the practice of farmers in the 1860s to have a doctor bleed them once a year, about the month of March for preference, in order to begin the spring with fresh blood in the veins. Not long afterwards however, bleeding seems to have gone out of fashion. An inventory of Dr. MacMillan's books lists a treatise dated 1874 entitled *"The Destructive Practice of Bleeding &etc"*

The shortcomings of the new school were minor compared with its predecessor. The children now had a far better environment in which to learn. The school room was relatively spacious and well lit and had proper desks. No longer did they have to carry the fire cage out of a smoke filled classroom when the wind was in the wrong direction. In fact their facilities were for a while equal to those of the parish school in the village. The school room was also an asset outside of school hours and like the old school was used for dancing in the evening and as a meeting place for the community.

A year or so after moving into his new house, on the evening of December 31, 1864, dominie Daniel Ferguson set out to walk across the moor to Devol farm, presumably intending to visit a friend to celebrate Hogmanay. He never arrived. The cold weather and exposed moor were too much for the 66 year old man, and he collapsed and died by the side of the farm track. His body was found the following day. Dominie Donald MacDonald, registrar of births marriages and deaths and fellow teacher in the parish recorded his death as having taken place on either December 31 or January 1st. No-one knew whether Daniel Ferguson lived to see the New Year of 1865.

The social advances that came with the Victorian age

right: The new subscription school (a digital reconstruction based on later photographs and specifications of building extensions).

The Side School

were to bring more change to the school. Less than ten years after the new school was opened, the Education (Scotland) Act of 1872 came into being. This was to have far-reaching effects by making education available and compulsory for all children between the ages of 5 and 13. The Side school was about to be taken into the new mainstream system of education.

The Act specified that every parish and burgh was to be constituted as a school district. A School Board was to be elected in each district, and the board was required to ensure that there was sufficient accommodation to meet the educational needs of all the children of school age. The key clause in the Act was the Compulsory Clause, which specified that every parent was obliged to ensure that his or her children between the ages of 5 and 13 were taught Reading, Writing and Arithmetic. Education was not free, but poverty was no excuse for keeping children at home. Needy parents could apply to the Parochial board of the parish for assistance in paying school fees. The Compulsory clause differed from that of the corresponding Education Act in England, where the enforcement of the Compulsory Clause was at the discretion of the district board. There was no such discretion in Scotland.

Chapter Five
Side Becomes a Public School
1874

As a result of the Education (Scotland) Act of 1872, a School Board was established in the parish, and they took over the management of the parish school. The School Board first met in April 1873. They had barely got to grips with their new responsibilities before the Reverend James Fyfe appeared at a board meeting, exactly one month after their first meeting. With the consent of the Side management committee, he offered to turn over the entire operation of the Side school to the new School Board. They attached a condition that the teacher they had recently hired, William Campbell, should continue in office.

The decision of the Side management committee to transfer control of the school to the School Board would not have been a difficult one to come to. Until now they had been solely responsible for the management and finance of the school as well as the employment of the teacher. By making it a public school the funding would be taken care of by central government grants and local taxes (though they would continue to pay school fees), and the problems of management and upkeep of the school and the employment of the teacher would be taken out of their hands, allowing them to get on with their jobs as farmers. Nevertheless, they must have felt some reluctance about losing control of their school that they had founded and nurtured over the years.

The School Board had already had a survey carried out, listing all the children in the parish of school age (between 5 and 13 years according to the definition in the Act) and showing where they lived, so they could easily assess whether there was sufficient capacity in the parish to provide education for all the children. The survey showed that of the 330 children in the parish, 195 were attending school. Sixteen were at Side (an unusually small roll for this period of the school's existence), 106 were at the parish school, 15 received private tuition and the remainder were at schools in neighbouring parishes at Bridge of Weir, Greenock, Port Glasgow and Langbank. The Side children were:

John (7) son of Mrs. M Blair of Branchal:

Archibald (8) son of William Caldwell of Newton:

William (12), Robert (11), Jessie (9) and Agnes (7) children of Alexander Graham of Blackwater:

Alexander (12) and Magdalen (10) children of Alexander McDougall of Dippany, a school manager:

James (9) and David (7) children of John Carson of Milton:

Mary Gibb (12), niece of James Baxter of Burnbank:

John (9) son of M Yuill of Carsemuir:

Jamie (7) son of William Love of Cairncurren:

Helen (8) daughter of Alexander Smillie of Clachers:

Duncan (12) and James (10) sons of Donald Ferguson of Hardridge.

There were also 4 boys and 2 girls in these families who were of school age but were not attending school.

The board then surveyed the Side building itself to see whether work was needed to bring it up to the standards required of a public school. William Campbell supplied a sketch ground plan showing the size of the plot. Even he, as a teacher, failed to calculate the area correctly from his measurements when using the awkward units of poles[1], yards and feet. Mr. Robert Knox, an officer of the board, was instructed to report on the sanitary condition of the buildings. He reported that there were *"no conveniences there whether for boys or girls. The buildings in other respects are in*

---

[1] *There are 160 poles to the acre*

excellent condition".

The board also took advice from their masters, the Scottish Education board, or more correctly, the Scotch Education board as it was then known. The main interests of this board appeared to be about segregation of the boys and girls. Their questionnaire demanded to know for example whether there were *"separate approaches"* to the boys and girls lavatories. The School Board did not trouble to respond to this point since there were no lavatories. Also, the external doors had to be arranged so that the boys and girls doors should lead into their respective playgrounds, and the infants door should lead into the girls playground. Evidently they believed that the younger children should not be unnecessarily exposed to the rowdy ways of the older boys.

There was also guidance about teachers. For a regular type of elementary day school, the boys were to be taught by a master, and the girls and infants by a mistress.

"To every 5 boys there will commonly be 4 girls and 6 infants. A smaller room will be required to separate the infants from the other children. If the one principal teacher be a master, a woman shall be required for the girls sewing and she should be able to teach the infants also. If the one principal teacher is a mistress she should have a pupil teacher to assist her".

Just why they anticipated fewer girls than boys when the Education Act stipulated compulsory education for all is not clear.

Taking all this information and guidelines into account, the School Board eventually decided that they needed the capacity of the Side school to meet the needs of the parish, but a number of alterations would be required to the building. A second classroom for the girls would have to be built, together with two play sheds, one for the boys and one for the girls. The play sheds were needed to give protection to the children at playtime when the weather was inclement (as it frequently was). Separate water closets for boys and girls were needed and a layout was devised so that the access to the girls WC was via the girls play shed, and the access to the boys WC was via the boys play shed, thus satisfying the Scottish Education boards requirement for *"separate approaches"*. The lavatory facilities that were eventually provided were in fact no more than a couple of buckets in a small lean-to building. An entrance porch was to be added with the intent of separating the boys entrances from that of the infants and girls, though in the event only one door was actually provided so that the instructions of the Scotch Education board to separate the sexes and separate the younger and older children were not complied with. Mrs. Lillias Laird from Mountblow, just a half mile along the road from the school, was engaged to teach the girls sewing and knitting for an hour and a half, three times a week. The possibility that boys would want to learn to sew or for that matter that a male teacher could teach sewing did not of course even cross anyone's mind.

Additional land was to be purchased so as to provide separate playgrounds for the boys and girls, retaining a small garden plot for the teacher, and the school house was to be improved by converting the loft area into two bedrooms. Finally the board decided to purchase the land on which the school and schoolhouse stood, instead of renting as had been the case until now.

The total cost of enlarging the school and schoolhouse and purchasing the enlarged plot of land was £676. Mr. Peter Woodrow from Bridge of Weir carried out the masonry work and Mr. Peter MacKay of Houston carried out the slating, plastering and plumbing. The Clerk to the School Board was instructed to apply for a 25 year loan from the Public Loan Commissioners for £2000 to cover the cost of the work and land at Side together with the cost of work on the village school that was also to be enlarged. By December 1873 the School Board formally assumed responsibility for Side, and this was ratified by the Scotch Education board in January 1874. The school was now called *"West Side Public School"*.

There was quite a delay in drawing up detailed plans for the alterations and getting them approved by the Scotch Education board in Edinburgh, so that the work of extending the school was not carried out until the summer of 1875. The school closed at the end of July, earlier than usual, to allow the workmen to start. They allowed only a little less than 2 months for the work, planning to finish on September 24 but in the event could not open the school until two weeks later. It was a difficult time for the teacher, impatient at the loss of teaching time, and even when the school eventually

right: The Westside Public School c1919, looking very much as it would after the rebuilding in 1875.

The Side School

opened, they were continually distracted by painters and other workmen finishing off the work

The detailed specifications of the school extensions survive, describing everything from the thirty black coat hooks, six new desks with iron standards at £2 each, Quebec yellow pine flooring and a Spanish mahogany handrail in the house, to the dressed stone from Whitespot quarry in Ayrshire.

Soon after completion of the work at Side, the School Board received another petition, this time from the residents at neighbouring Glenmill. There had been a school at Glenmill that was flourishing in the 1850s but had now fallen into disuse, presumably through lack of pupils. The residents realised that government money was in the offing, and asked the board to reinstate this school, pointing out that it would need very little expense to make it operational again. The School Board lost no time in turning down this application however, believing that two schools was quite sufficient to meet the needs of the parish. The petition was turned down on the grounds that some of the petitioners lived outside the parish, some had no children and the remainder lived a reasonable distance from existing schools, so the school at Glenmill was never re-opened.

One of the disciplines imposed on the new West Side Public School was the need to keep a log book, in which the teacher wrote a brief account of the activities of each week. The original log books for Side have survived and are kept in the Glasgow City Archives, where we can read the teacher's first - though not particularly memorable - entry, written on January 8, 1875 in his best copperplate script:

"The school not in regular working order owing to New Year Holidays"

Chapter Six
The School Board

The School Board of the Parish of Kilmacolm was an elected body of 5 people, serving a 3 year term of office. Their job was to implement the Education (Scotland) Act of 1872 to provide compulsory education for all of the children in the parish between the ages of 5 and 13. The first board election in 1873 was uncontested. The heritors had got together and decided between themselves on 5 candidates, and no other names were put forward. There was nothing sinister in this. They were not the kind of people to spend money unnecessarily and were merely trying to save the expense and effort of holding an election. They tried to do the same thing at subsequent elections but without success. By the time of the second election the community were familiar with the new legislation. They were genuinely interested in the education of their children and the office of School Board member was regarded as prestigious. Future elections were hotly contested.

Women were eligible for election to the board, and married women were able to vote. The boards were in fact the first major political forum for women. In contrast more than fifty years were to pass before all women over the age of 21 were able to vote in parliamentary elections. However in 1873 the cause of equal rights for women was not uppermost in the minds of the somewhat conservative electorate of the parish of Kilmacolm, and throughout the entire history of the Kilmacolm School Board only one woman was ever elected - Isabel Barr - who sat on the board between 1906 and 1913.

Members of the first board were:

> Sir Michael Robert Shaw-Stewart, Lord Lieutenant of the County of Renfrewshire. He was appointed chairman of the School Board.
>
> Thomas Thoms, a farmer of Auchenbothie farm
>
> George Wood, a merchant. He was one of the new class of commuters, resident in Kilmacolm and working in Glasgow, making use of the new railway service that had started in Kilmacolm four years previously in 1869.
>
> Robert Lindsay, a bookseller, who like George Wood commuted to his work in Glasgow.
>
> Frederick Bryan, a factor. A factor managed landed property, letting farms, collecting rents and paying salaries. He was an influential person in the parish.

Later on as the population of the parish increased, the size of the board was increased to 7 members. A typical board composition was two ministers, two farmers and two business men or merchants, with Sir Michael's factor, as chairman. After 1887, no more farmers were elected, demonstrating the way the population of the parish was changing as the professional and merchant classes started to invade the village, seeing Kilmacolm as a desirable place of residence, and commuting to their place of work on the train. Their occupations were widely varied, and over the years School Board members included a glass manufacturer, linen merchant, iron master, silk throwster, commercial traveller, architect, stockbroker, engineer, surgeon, chemist, leather merchant, cabinet maker and a clothier.

One could be forgiven for having low expectations of the success of the first board. They were a part time, unpaid body, with no previous experience of school management. The job they had taken on was a major one. The idea of compulsory education for everyone between the ages of 5 and 13 was novel, and not every farmer took kindly to the idea that his son might not be available to work on the farm at busy times.

In spite of he fact that the board members frequently behaved in a pompous and inflexible manner, and constantly got involved in all sorts of squabbles amongst themselves, they managed to do an effective job. In their first term of office they undertook major rebuilding programs in both the village school and at Side. They were responsible for the employment of the teachers and fixing and collecting school fees. They summoned the parents of truant children to appear before them, cajoling them to mend their ways under threat of the law. They dealt with poor people who were unable to afford school fees. They fixed the school holidays, purchased and presented prizes at the end of term and took an interest in the moral and spiritual welfare of the children as well as their educational needs.

The board met about twice a month, holding meetings alternately in the village school and at the chambers of George Wood in Frederick Street, Glasgow. Imagine travelling all the way to Glasgow just to attend a meeting! One can imagine Farmer Thoms reflecting as he sat on the train steaming at speed to Glasgow that barely a decade earlier such a journey would have been unthinkable. After the death of George Wood in April 1877, meetings were held only at the Kilmacolm School.

Luckily there are comprehensive records of the work of the School Board, and the original School Board minute books survive in the Glasgow City Archives. As well as minutes of their meetings, the books contain transcripts of each letter sent out and received by the board, forming in total a comprehensive record that would put many modern businesses to shame. Towards the end of their three year period of office they held a public meeting to report on their achievements. These meetings were well attended lively affairs and reported in detail in the Greenock and Paisley newspapers. At the first of these public meetings the secrecy of School Board meetings was condemned, and from then on board meetings were open to the press and were frequently reported in detail in the *Greenock Telegraph* and the *Paisley and Renfrewshire Gazette*.

Sir Michael Robert Shaw-Stewart, chairman of the first board, did not actually attend a single meeting, being far too busy with his parliamentary work to give time to the School Board. He probably assumed that his factor would represent him at meetings as he did in meetings of the heritors, but this was not allowed in the case of School Boards. He accordingly submitted his resignation, but the Scotch Education Department would not accept it, stating that they did not accept resignations

6: The School Board

Rev Dr. James Murray, Parish Minister and School Board member from 1879 to 1918

Horatio R B Peile, factor to Sir Michael Shaw-Stewart and School Board Chairman from 1874 to 1916

Rev Thos Gregory, Free Church Minister and School Board member from 1898 to 1913

Rev James Fyfe, United Presbyterian minister, chairman of the Subscription School management committee and School Board member from 1879 to 1898

"at pleasure" and required a serious reason such as ill-health or death(!). Sir Michael accordingly resigned on the grounds of ill-health and the board dutifully appointed his factor, Mr. Horatio Renaud Babington Peile, in his place.

Mr. Peile served on the board from 1874 until his death in 1916, for most of the time as chairman. He was also chairman of the parochial board. He was an effective chairman, and his skills in running meetings were often called on. Board meetings were lively affairs with much posturing and disagreement among the members. They had certainly not got their act together in 1876 as the *Paisley and Renfrewshire Gazette* reported under the heading: "A Scene at a Supper Party"

> "On Tuesday evening last the Kilmacolm Choral Society held their annual Concert with George Wood in the chair. Arrangements were made for supper and dancing afterwards with the permission of two members of the board. Mr. Thoms of Auchenbothie farm and a member of the School Board appeared in a state of nervous excitement and declared without consulting any of the other board members that he would not allow a supper or dancing in the school room and he proceeded to put out the gas. The master of the school then attacked the committee personally in an abusive manner. The committee decided to postpone the dance, some of them having travelled a considerable distance to be there."

The following month saw the end of the term of office of the board and for the first time an election took place for a new board. Each elector had five votes that could be used as desired, either one vote each for five different candidates, or if preferred all five votes could be awarded to one candidate. The election was a lively affair, as reported in the *Greenock Telegraph*:

The Side School

1876
The Greenock Telegraph and Clyde Shipping Gazette

KILMACOLM SCHOOL BOARD ELECTION- The polling took place yesterday and caused considerable stir. A large flag was suspended from Stewart Place, to which was attached posters asking the electors to vote for Mr. Thoms and Thomson, as the favourite candidates. Squibs were also used on some of the candidates, the farmers being told to vote for Peile and to remember that he was factor. Wood was said to be woo(-)d but not won; electors were asked to vote for dancing boots and stock lugs &etc., &etc. A cartoon representing Peile, Thoms and Thomson far up on a pole, and the feet downwards was also exhibited- one of them at the foot exclaiming "Down with the impostors". It seemed clear from the beginning that Peile and Thoms would be far ahead, doubts being expressed as to the position the others would hold. At 6 pm the results were declared as under:-

H. R. B. Peile (Episcopalian)	398
Thomas S Thoms (UP)	375
John Thomson (EC)	117
George Wood (EC)	112
A C Stevenson (UP)	39

Messrs. Peile, Thoms, and Wood were members of the old board. The unsuccessful were- Robt. Lindsay, Baptist, 86, a member of the old board, and John Hunter, 27, a new candidate. There were 13 spoiled papers. Walter Holms Esq. was returning officer, assisted by Jas. Miller Esq., writer, Paisley, and Messrs. Alex Robertson and Thomas Rowan, clerks. There are 380 names on the valuation roll and a goodly number came from Greenock and Port Glasgow to record their votes. The flag having been transferred to the ground in front of the schoolhouse, the returning officer made the declaration amid loud cheering. Mr. Peile thanked the electors for the proud position they had placed him in, and said that, with the assistance of his old colleagues and the new members, he was sure that the educational wants of the parish would be attended to with efficiency and economy. Messrs. Thoms, Thomson and Wood, who were also warmly received, expressed their thanks. An attempt was made to drive Mr. Peile through the village, but he managed to get away. Mr. Thoms, however was caught, and driven through the streets.

6: The School Board

Chapter Seven
William Campbell
1873 to 1877

When Daniel Ferguson died in at the end of 1863 he was succeeded by Rob Robertson, about whom little is known except that he was a 25 year old bachelor. In 1873 the school management committee appointed William Campbell as teacher, and he saw the school through the difficult period of the transition from subscription school to public school.

William Campbell was born in Caithness in the Highlands of Scotland, starting his teaching career in 1844 at the age of 19, probably in his home county. After teaching there for three years he realised that formal qualifications would be necessary to further his career so he travelled south to Glasgow to take a two year course, gaining his teacher's certificate in December 1871. There were two training colleges in Glasgow: a Church of Scotland college and a Free Church college, as well as one in Edinburgh. William Campbell graduated from The Glasgow Free Church College and took up his first appointment as a certificated teacher at the Port Glasgow Free Church School, a few miles from the village of Kilmacolm. After a year or so at Port Glasgow he took up his position at Side, no doubt being attracted by the prospect of being his own boss after his experience as an assistant at Port Glasgow, albeit at a tiny country school. He was first appointed by the management committee of the subscription school and at the insistence of the management committee, retained his post when Side became a public school.

So how did the transition from subscription school to public school affect the children and their teacher at the school? At first sight not very much. There were material changes of course in the school buildings, but the fact that there were now separate playgrounds for the boys and girls would hardly be of great significance- they were surrounded by open country with hills, rocks and streams that made an ideal natural play area. More important was the new equipment that was obtained for the school:

> *Maps of Europe, Asia, Africa, the United States of America and South America, and relief maps of Renfrewshire, Scotland, Ireland and England;*
>
> *Drawing specimens;*
>
> *Wall sheets of objects in natural history;*
>
> *A school clock;*
>
> *A blackboard;*
>
> *Reading books.*

These items may not seem impressive by today's standards, but remember that until this time the equipment available to the teacher was little more than a Bible and a leather strap. Many of the children had not seen such maps before, neither apparently did they have the benefit of a blackboard in the subscription school.

The maps were in a way symbolic of a more outward-looking attitude in the school. Some time later a map of the British Empire was hung in central position in front of the class above the fireplace, showing an ever-expanding area of pink.

On April 29, 1876 a short and not at all prominent paragraph in the *Greenock Telegraph* recorded that Queen Victoria had decided to assume the title *"Empress of India"*.

Because the school was now part of a national education system, they began to get attention from Her Majesty's Inspectors. They carried out formal annual inspections followed up with a written report to the School Board. Children were now being assessed on the basis of national standards, and would get the benefit of any new advances in educational techniques that were developed. The inspections were also important because the school was now receiving grants which were assessed in part on the basis of the number of pupils reaching the required grade in each standard.

One subject that Her Majesty's Inspectors did not examine was the Scriptures, which was specifically excluded by the Education Act. This was the start of a gradual reduction in the degree of influence exerted by the Church on education, although the church still ran the teachers training colleges and continued to do so until 1905. Also the clergy were usually well represented on School Boards, but unusually the Kilmacolm board did not have a minister until the third board election in 1879 when the Reverend James Murray and the Reverend James Fyfe were elected. The clergy continued to be represented until the management of schools was taken over by the County Education Authority in 1919. Although the bible continued to be well used in schools, the children learned to read using books designed for that purpose (the *Royal Reader*) rather than the bible and catechism which were far less suitable for that purpose.

The school also had visits from the local gentry. The school log book school shows that Lady Octavia Shaw-Stewart, wife of Sir Michael Shaw-Stewart the Lord Lieutenant of the County (and chairman of the first School Board) started to visit the school to listen to reading classes and examine the girls' sewing. The Shaw-Stewarts had three residences in the county at that time, one of them Duchal House, a mile or two from the Side school. Lady Octavia was a well known benefactor in the neighbourhood as described by the Paisley and Renfrewshire Gazette in their rather unctuous report of January 1875:

> *"Lady Octavia Shaw-Stewart well known for her kindness and attention to the poor on the estates of which her husband the popular Lord Lieutenant is proprietor visited the public school and kindly distributed her annual donation of warm clothing to the recipients of her bounty in the village and neighbourhood".*

In later years Lady Octavia made it her practice to visit Side at Christmas. It must have been quite an occasion for the children when she drove up in her carriage, joined in the children's party and gave each of the children a Christmas gift. Mrs. Jessie McLeod still has a silver button hook give by Lady Octavia to her mother, Elizabeth Crawford, in the 1890s. This kind of attention would have had the effect of giving the children a wider vision, making them feel much less remote from the world outside.

The parents also found themselves in a completely different situation. In the days of the Subscription School they struggled to provide funds for the school and the teacher to ensure that their children got an education. Though they were now relieved of the responsibility of paying for the school building and teachers salary (though they still had to pay school fees), they must have found it galling to discover that if they kept their children away from school to help on the farm at busy times the authorities were quick to point out the error of their ways, under threat of the law.

For the teacher there was even more change, with regular external inspections and a new employer- the School Board. Every year he would offer his services anew to the board, sometimes asking for an increase in salary. Security of employment was not a privilege he enjoyed. As we shall see later, the board had no compunction in terminating the teacher's employment if they felt it to be advantageous, regardless of how good a job the teacher was doing.

Until this time the teacher had been a single man. Now the extensions to the school house meant that there was accommodation for a married couple with children in reasonable comfort by the standards of the time. Nor need the teacher be a man. The Scotch Education board had decreed that women were capable - even preferred to men - for teaching infants, expressing the view that if children *"are brought under the gentler, more natural qualities of female teachers, a better result may be attained than if trained entirely by men"*. Women teachers however were usually subordinate to a male head teacher, and they were paid about half as much as male teachers. A married woman however was out of the question: married women were definitely not expected to work. In any event Kilmacolm was not yet ready for a female teacher, whether married or not.

William Campbell seems to have been a rather private man. His entries in the school log book were terse, giving away little about his character. We know that he was unmarried and that he suffered from asthma. On one occasion he was summoned before the School Board to explain his absence for a week during which time the school was closed. He explained that he had been confined to bed with asthma and was instructed

The Side School

that *"in future he must intimate to the School Board clerk any occasion on which he might be absent or the school closed"*, a rather unsympathetic response to a man living alone in a rather remote place, without the assistance of a telephone to communicate with the board. He seems to have been well thought of as a teacher, the management committee of the subscription school making his continued employment a condition of handing the school over to the School Board. The reports received from Her Majesty's Inspectors in 1876 and 1877 were also favourable: In 1876:

"This school is very well conducted and the results shewn at the examination were very commendable in all respects. The erection of a classroom is nearly completed and other improvements are being carried out on the premises"

and in 1877:

"The school is taught with much fidelity and on the whole with creditable success. The grant for comprehension of lessons and grammar (Art 19C1) is rather barely secured. History and geography are very fair. The order and general tone are good"

HMI were less impressed with the village school, or at any rate with their educational achievements. Their report for the village school, also in 1877, said:

"The new school is one of the most handsome and best furnished in the county ... on the whole the educational results are not satisfactory ... in the fourth standard, nearly all the children failed reading writing and arithmetic".

William Campbell's salary in his first year under the School Board was £70 per annum, only a few pounds more than assistant teachers in the village school. This was increased to £75 in 1876 and £85 in 1877. He also got fees from evening classes that he ran in winter months. Donald MacDonald, head teacher at the village school got about £180 in the same period.

Most of his log book entries are concerned with attendance and the difficulty in preparing the children for annual inspections. There were frequent absences because of bad weather and sickness - *"scarlet fever and measles in the district"* was a common entry. The older boys were frequently absent to attend ploughing matches in January, sowing corn in March, setting potatoes in April, attending the Greenock cattle show in June and harvesting in September. They were also absent for the Kilmacolm cattle show, but that was such an important event that a vacation was given. The Compulsory Officer was kept hard at work to persuade parents that school attendance really was compulsory. In the first week of June 1876 the weather was obviously bright and sunny as William Campbell wrote in his log:

> *"Attendance less this week, parents and children away pleasure seeking"*

In addition to all of these problems he had to close the school early in the summer of 1875 to allow the building work associated with the change to public school status to proceed, and in the following term was inconvenienced by workmen and painters in the school room. It must have been a difficult period. The efforts of the compulsory officer meant that the roll had now increased, so that William Campbell was now teaching 46 children, with ages varying from five to thirteen, assisted only by Mrs. Lillias Laird who taught the girls sewing for three or four hours a week. This pupil to teacher ratio was within the requirements of the Education Act however, which specified one teacher for up to sixty children.

The compulsory officer, Donald Simpson, visited each of the two schools in the parish once a week and got from the teachers the names of children who were not attending. He then called on the parents to find out why their children were not attending and if there was no satisfactory reason given, reported the parents to the board. In some cases, non-attendance was because the parents were not able to pay the school fees, and in these cases the School Board clerk might apply to the Parochial Board for payment of school fees. In one case the officer reported that *"a delicate boy could not attend school because he had no boots"*. The officer soon got some boots for him by writing to the Inspector of Poor, a nice example of effective welfare support for the needy with a minimum of bureaucracy. It had previously been established that in cases when the parish paid school fees, the needy parishioners were not automatically branded as paupers, so that people could apply for assistance with school fees without risking this dreaded stigma.

There were however cases of non-attendance that the board did not find acceptable, especially where children of school age were being employed. For example:

> *"Mr. John Hunter, farmer at Dykfoot has a boy*

The Side School

belonging to David Millar shoemaker for at least two months".

Offending parents were summoned to appear before the School Board and given a severe warning. If this was not effective the matter would be referred to the Procurator Fiscal. The first case in Kilmacolm was a Mr. McGinty who ignored the ticking off he got from the board and was later was fined 10/6 (52p) plus expenses of 10/6, both of which he immediately paid. It was not a course of action that the School Board liked to follow however, because they had to pay the expenses of the prosecution, in this case £4-12-4 (£4.20).

***

The increase in the school roll from 16 to 46 in the space of only three years must have been largely as a consequence of the Education Act and the introduction of compulsory education. The interpretation of these figures is probably not so much that the number of children receiving formal education increased almost threefold, but that children now stayed at school for the whole of the period from the age of five to thirteen, rather than staying for just long enough to learn the basics of reading and writing, maybe supplemented by a few weeks of evening class in the winter.

On October 13, 1877, William Campbell's entry in the Side school log book was as usual short and to the point:

"Attendance small. Services of the present teacher close today".

He did not even sign his name. He had accepted a new post at the public school of Swiney, a tiny village in the Highlands not far from Wick. Perhaps he was homesick and had been scanning the newspapers for job vacancies that would give him the opportunity to return to the county of Caithness where he was born.

7: William Campbell: 1873 to 1877

Chapter Eight
Stewart Archibald
1877 to 1884

Following William Campbell's resignation, the School Board advertised for a male certificated teacher in *The Glasgow Herald, The Northern British Daily, The Glasgow News, The Scotsman, The Greenock Telegraph, The Ayr Advertiser, The Johnston Gleaner, The Johnstonian,* and *The Dundee Advertiser.* There was a good response, a short list of candidates was selected for interview, and Stewart Archibald was appointed. His salary was £75 per annum with the school house and garden. He was also allowed to keep the fees for evening classes that were run in the winter months. He was paid one guinea to cover his expenses while attending for interview - his rail fare from Irvine and his accommodation at the Aitkins Temperance Hotel in Glasgow.

Stewart Archibald was trained at Edinburgh in 1864 and 1865. His previous school was at Perceton by Irvine, a few miles North of Irvine. He was 32 years old, a married man with two sons, both preparing to attend Glasgow University. His wife Mary gave birth to a daughter Louisa after they had been at Side for about a year. In April 1878, when Mrs. Lillias Laird moved from Mountblow to the village, Mary Archibald took over as sewing mistress.

8: Stewart Archibald 1877 to 1884

Throughout Stewart Archibald's period at the school, disciplinary matters figured prominently, as is evident from both the school log and the School Board minutes. In his second month he reported:

"had a "row" with a big boy because he did not stay in when he had failed in his lesson, and refused next day to submit to his punishment for his fault. In the end he had to yield"

The punishment the boy eventually yielded to was the tawse, a leather strap cut into strips at the business end. Though Scotland can be proud of the extent to which education was made available to all classes from very early times, the use of the tawse, which continued until the middle of the twentieth century was not something to be proud of. What made it particularly iniquitous was that children were strapped not just for disciplinary matters, but because of their poor performance in their lessons, as if a beating would improve their intellectual achievement.

On this occasion the boy's father complained to the School Board, and the board summoned the teacher to attend a board meeting to explain his actions. In the event, the board were lenient and cautioned Mr. Archibald "as to his acting in the future so as to prevent any further complaints being made to the board". The board were evidently more concerned about being bothered by complaints of this kind than they were about the welfare of the children.

Stewart Archibald must have been unpopular with the board because of the never ending stream of letters he fired off to them, mostly about alterations and repairs required to the school house. For example in January 1878:

"In regard to the dwelling house - the plasterer sent some material a good while ago with which to execute some repairs but has not been here to do the work. Till this is done we cannot put the bedroom in order. The parlour is very damp so much so that anything we have put in it becomes spoiled. The vent draws so badly that we cannot put on a fire. Will the School Board kindly try some remedies soon as possible. I have to provide the kitchen grate with a slider below price 3s - 9d. I am also to put up 4 drying poles on the green price to be about

right: fragments from Stewart Archibald's log book

The Side School

Dec 14th Attendance about the same. Work carried on as usual, with little change from usual routine. Had a "row" with a big boy because he did not stay in when he had failed in his lesson, and refused next day to submit to punishment for his fault. In the [end had] to yield. Received [...] sent by the [...] Edinburgh, in which [...] information [...] for year ending Dec 31st 18[..] [...] somewhat less th[an] Work carried on much [...] attention paid to arith[metic] [...]roaching examination [...] Thursday afternoon [mem]ber of School Board

Log Book.

1877. Decr 28th This week the amount of useful work done in the school has been much below par, Tuesday being Christmas day, some half dozen were absent on that account. A severe snowstorm set in on Tuesday night, lasting the rest of the week, and reducing the attendance by one half.

1878. Jany 4th Tuesday being New Year's day, that and the following day were given as holidays. That and the low attendance (from [...]) the ordinary atten[dance]

6/-. Will the School Board defray the expense so that they will remain there permanently?"

In response, the board agreed to supply a stove for the parlour. Then in 1882:

"I am informed by Mr. Love of Margarets Mill farm that he intends putting potatoes in the field immediately behind the school - the field from which the supply of water for the school and the school house is obtained. Of course a large quantity of manure of various kinds will be put in the field and the water will of necessity become so much contaminated thereby that it will be rendered entirely unfit for use. I have therefore humbly and respectfully to lay before the School Board the desirability - the necessity - of introducing a supply of pure water before the existing supply shall have been rendered unfit for use.

A number of attempts were made to improve the water supply over the years, but a reliable supply was never provided throughout the entire history of the school until its closure in 1951.

In the 1880s the School Board received a number of requests for the use of the school facilities for various types of event, mostly for the village school but a few for the Side school. They received requests for the use of the village school for:

Concerts, including one by the Kilmacolm Orchestral Society;

A lecture entitled "Free Emigration to New Zealand";

A working mens club course of lectures;

A lecture and exhibition of accompanying panorama by a Mr. Hall, a lecturer on Africa;

A series of lectures on behalf of the Kilmacolm Young Mens Christian Association;

Donald MacDonald, head teacher at the village school and superintendent of the Band of Hope, now transformed into Juvenile Good Templar Lodge under the name The Morning Star of Kilmacolm with a membership 104 children requested the use of a classroom.

Not all of the applications were agreed to, and the board did not appear to have any consistent policy as to what they would or would not accept. At first they permitted use of the school for dancing classes, but at a later date withdrew permission on the grounds that

The Side School

dancing classes were *"not conducive to morality"*. They had no hesitation in rejecting an application from the agent of the *Blondinette Minstrels* of Westbourne Grove, Bayswater, London for use of the village school for a concert. *"I am not at all satisfied that a company such as this should be encouraged at all"* was their comment. One wonders just what real or imaginary threat to public morality was posed by the *Blondinette Minstrels*. Perhaps they had heard reports of their performances elsewhere in the county.

The board were happy to approve an application by Mr. Barr for the use of the West Side school room for an hour each week on Savings Bank purposes without charge. Also welcome were the Glasgow Evangelical Union Sabbath School Teachers Association. The Paisley and Renfrewshire Gazette reported on June 10 1876:

> *"The EU Sabbath School Teachers Association visited Kilmacolm intending to visit the romantic ruin at old Duchal but were prevented from doing so by heavy rain. Mr. MacDonald allowed them to use the school room where interesting addresses and musical selections were given"*

The ruins of Duchal Castle are less than a mile from the Side school, and the Sabbath School Teachers Association were given permission to use the Side school as a base for future visits.

Kilmacolm was now becoming a favourite spot for weekend outings for people in the surrounding towns. In July 1876 the Paisley and Renfrewshire Gazette reported:

> *"Pic-nics: On Saturday between 1500 and 2000 persons visited the vicinity, the Buchanan Institute and the Maxwell Sabbath Schools and some Good Templar Lodges being the chief contingents"*

The Good Templar Lodges were organisations of the Temperance Movement.

By 1880 the upheaval of transferring the school from Subscription School to Public School and the implementation of the 1872 Education Act was effectively complete, attendance for 5 to 13 year old children was now the norm, and the school was able to settle into something of a routine, though the older boys still took odd days off to help with the farming work and the older girls were sometimes absent for child minding.

The children were taught reading, writing, arithmetic, history, geography and the scriptures, and the girls were also taught sewing. At the village school they had a more extensive syllabus and were earning grants for additional subjects like Music, Domestic Economy, English Literature, Physical Geography, Inorganic Chemistry, Animal Physiology, Freehand Drawing, Geometric Drawing, Perspective Drawing and Model Drawing. Stewart Archibald, running the school single handed (apart from his wife teaching sewing) could not cover such a variety of subjects. He did however manage to find time to include a little poetry and singing into the timetable, though his technique for teaching recitation would not endear him to the class:

26/7/78: "*gave the classes some poetry to say today. Very fairly done*".

2/8/78: "*recitation better. They got each the same piece to say again and to do so until perfect*".

31/12/78: "*...during most of the year have taught singing nearly every day for 10 minutes or so after calling the roll*"

Stewart Archibald's log shows that like his predecessor he had a never-ending struggle to prepare for school inspections in the face of absences due to severe weather, epidemics that struck from time to time, and absences for farming work. In March 1881:

"*..on Thursday afternoon a terrific snowstorm came on lasting all night and all Friday with very little cessation. Heavy fall and much drifting. Two boys appeared on Friday. No appearance of abatement in the storm*".

Not a single child appeared at the start of the following week because all of the roads were blocked by snow.

In June everyone got a day off on the Wednesday of the cattle show, but a number of the boys stretched the holiday to the end of the week:

"*Holiday on Wednesday- Kilmacolm cattle show. 14 absent next day. Of these 9 were present on Friday and on being questioned gave sore heads, sore throats etc as the reason of absence. Evidently the holiday and show had to do with it*"

The show itself lasted for only one day, but the boys clearly found entertainment that detained them longer, their sore heads presumably being a clue. The following year there was a similar comment in the log, and one can sense the teacher's exasperation:

The Side School

"several absent on Thursday and Friday as always happens on such occasions which I say is outrageous!"

To make it worse, the week after the Kilmacolm show was the Greenock show:

"At least 5 absent at Greenock show "taking sheep, dogs etc thereto"

In May 1878:

"Today was the Queens birthday. It seems the Kilmacolm Public School is closed and the scholars in the morning were asking for a holiday here. Being all assembled I would not send them away again but said I would give them next Friday instead. Three absented themselves in the afternoon without leave"

Just before the Summer holidays in August, there was a short examination and prize-giving in the presence of some of the School Board members and parents. In 1878 the teacher was given a cheque for £1.50 with which to buy prizes. Prizes were awarded on the basis of attendance rather than on successful examination results. On August 13 1878:

"The examination and closing of the school formerly arranged for tomorrow took place today uniform with the other school which had to be closed today in consequence of its being required for ceremonies in connection with the waterworks for Kilmacolm and it was thought better to have both examinations on the same day. Attendance 45. Present Mr. Thoms, Thomson of the School Board and a few parents and others, almost entirely females. Mr. Thoms distributed the prizes and he and Mr. Thomson each said a few appropriate words to the children"

The following year the Reverend Murray who was now on the School Board presented the prizes:

"The Rev Murray expressed himself as well pleased and presented the prizes and gift books, every child getting a book. Six prizes given to most regular attendees. School closed until 7th October"

Elizabeth Stewart got the first prize in 1883 having had a full attendance record for the previous 18 months.

School holidays were rather shorter than is usual nowadays. In 1878 they got 6 weeks in the summer and two days at Hogmanay. There was no holiday at Easter nor on Christmas day, though on December 28 1877 the log entry was:

> "*Tuesday being Christmas day some half dozen were absent on that account*"

In the 1880's the holidays were gradually increased. The Summer holiday was increased to about 8 weeks, 4 days were given at Easter, Christmas day was a holiday and a week was given at Hogmanay.

The teacher himself was absent in June 1882, having to give evidence in the prosecution of Mr. Donald Ferguson whose child was not attending school. The journey would have taken all day, and Mr. Archibald must have been particularly annoyed at having a wasted journey when on this occasion the case was withdrawn.

In 1883, all of the children in the parish were given a holiday and were entertained for tea in Kilmacolm Public School by Sir Michael and Lady Octavia Shaw-Stewart on the occasion of the marriage of their eldest son and heir.

***

In the village itself, improvements continued to take place. A gas supply had been provided in 1873, and in 1878 Sir Michael opened the new public water supply, marked by a fountain near the centre of the village. In the same year William Quarrier started educating children in the nearby Orphan Homes of Scotland. In 1880 a hydropathic establishment was established in the village.

The *Greenock Telegraph* reported faithfully the events of the village including School Board elections and School Board meetings, alongside national and international news items. There were innumerable wars in Europe and elsewhere, Britain being involved in her fair share of them. For example, on April 14 the *Greenock Telegraph* reported the death of General Gordon in Khartoum, the Anglo-Russian war, a rising in Canada, and the first meeting of the newly elected School Board of the parish of Kilmacolm!

Back at Side, throughout Stewart Archibald's time at the school, reports from Her Majesty's Inspectors continued to be good. For example in 1878 the inspector John Boyd found 41 pupils present when he examined the school and reported:

> "*The school is faithfully taught and is generally in*

The Side School

a very creditable state of efficiency. Some improvement in Geography and History is desirable, the pass rate in these subjects being rather bare ... the grant for Geography and History has been barely earned and my Lords will look for much better results next year ... The amount of grant earned for the year ended 21 December 1878 is £32-2s-0d."

The grant was calculated partly on the basis of average attendance and partly on the basis of the number of pupils in each grade passing in the subjects presented for examination. History and Geography never attracted favourable reports throughout the history of the school and they did not always receive a grant for those subjects. Other sources of income were school fees, with the balance coming from the parish education rate. School fees were still being paid, though children under 7 were free, and when more than 3 children in the same family attended, a not uncommon circumstance at that time, only three had to pay. On average parents paid about 60p annually per child for school fees.

In 1881 the balance sheet for Side was as shown below. The "To Balance" was met by a contribution from the parish rate.

Grant	£40 - 7 - 0	Teachers' salaries	£95- 0 - 0
School fees	£26 - 3 - 3	Books, apparatus and stationery	£1-10 - 0
		Fuel, lighting and cleaning	£8- 3 - 0
		Replacement of furniture, and repairs to building and furniture	£4- 1 - 6
		Rents, rates, taxes and insurance	£1- 1 -10
To Balance	£44 -16 - 1	Prizes - books	£1-10 - 0
Total	£111- 6 - 4	Total	£111- 6 - 4

KILMALCOLM SCHOOL BOARD.

Kilmalcolm and West-Side Schools were re-opened on Tuesday, 12th September, 1882.

STAFF OF KILMALCOLM PUBLIC SCHOOL—

MR. DONALD M'DONALD, Head Master.
MR. WILLIAM WALKER, Assistant.
MISS HELEN BOYD, Assistant.
AND THREE PUPIL TEACHERS.

STAFF OF WEST-SIDE SCHOOL—

MR. STEWART ARCHIBALD.
MRS. ARCHIBALD.

Fees Payable every 4 weeks in advance, on the following dates, from 9 to 10 a.m., in the Board Room, Kilmalcolm, viz:—

1882.				1883.						
September,	October,	November,	December,	January,	February,	March,	April,	April,	May,	June,
18th.	16th.	13th.	11th.	8th.	5th.	5th.	2nd.	30th.	28th.	25th.

The following Fees include all the ordinary branches, and also Music, Drawing, and Drill—

Children under 7 years—Infants, and STANDARD, I.	FREE.
STANDARDS II. and III.	1s. „ per month of 4 weeks.
STANDARDS IV. and V.	1s. 4d. „ „
STANDARD VI.	1s. 8d. „ „

Where Four or more Children, being members of the same Family, are regularly attending School, only the Three Youngest of those chargeable with Fees will be charged.

ADVANCED CLASSES.

If a sufficient number of Pupils come forward, it is proposed to form in Kilmalcolm Public School advanced classes for Latin, French, Mathematics, and the higher English Subjects; the Fee for which will be 2s. 6d. per month.

EVENING CLASSES.

Evening Classes will be conducted during the Winter Months, of the beginning of which due notice will be given. Fee for the Session of Four Months 5s.

BY ORDER OF THE BOARD.

H. R. B. PEILE,
CHAIRMAN.

Kilmalcolm, 15th September, 1882.

The Side School

During Stewart Archibald's stay at Side, new School Boards were elected in 1879, 1882 and 1885. In 1879 two ministers were elected to the board, the Reverend James Eckford Fyfe, formerly the chairman of the School Management Committee of Side when it was a subscription school, and the Reverend James Murray. Both of them were to have a long association with the School Board. James Fyfe was elected 5 times and was serving on the board at the time of his death in 1898. The Rev. Murray was elected 10 times and was a member of the last School Board that sat until 1919 when the School Board system came to an end.

The Rev. Murray often found himself in dispute with other members of the board, particularly with the chairman, Mr. Peile. The Rev. Murray was in favour of reducing and eventually abolishing school fees. He persuaded the board to reduce fees in 1879, but his proposals for further reductions in 1881 and 1882 were rejected. Some of the board members had been elected on the basis of promises of "economy and efficiency" and "reduced rates". These members and Mr. Peile in particular, representing the interests of Sir Michael Shaw-Stewart, the biggest ratepayer in the parish, were against any proposal to reduce school fees.

In 1882 the population of the parish had grown to 2700 which meant that the size of the new School Board was increased from five to seven members. One of the new board members had a bright idea for saving the rate-payers money, as a result of which in July 1884 the clerk was instructed to write to Mr. Archibald telling him that his services would no longer be required after the first of November.

This was devastating news to Stewart Archibald, a married man with three children, about to lose his job and his home. He asked the board several times why they were dismissing him, each time getting an evasive answer or being told it was on account of decreasing attendance at the school. Stewart Archibald suspected that the reason was the number of letters of complaint sent to the board about harsh discipline, and indeed there had been some complaints over the years. Things had started to go wrong at the school in 1884 with more than usual unauthorised absences and a number of the children being transferred from Side to the village school for no apparent reason. One senses that the teacher was losing the confidence of the parents. In the log book in April 1884 he wrote a revealing comment:

> *"The work drags wearily; all spirit seems to have gone out of it"*

The real reason for his dismissal however was nothing to do with his teaching or with matters of discipline. The board realised that they could hire a female teacher to do the same job and pay her only half as much. Stewart Archibald was getting £85 at this time and his wife got an additional £10 for sewing instruction. His successor was to get only £50 and teach sewing herself. It was a situation that showed up clearly the iniquity of unequal pay, both in bringing in a female teacher at an unfairly low salary, and in putting a man out of his job and his family out of their home.

The board advertised in *The Scotsman* and the *Glasgow Herald*:

Female Certificated teacher wanted immediately to take entire charge of a small school in Kilmacolm parish. Salary not less than £50 with good house and garden. Apply Rev J Murray, the Manse, Kilmacolm.

Nine

Annie Craig Bell
1884 to 1905

There were few jobs available for women in 1884, and when the School Board advertised for a female certificated teacher there were 38 applicants, a considerable number considering that the remote location of the school could hardly be thought to make the post attractive for a single woman. The candidates were of course all single women, it being unheard of for a married woman to work at this time. Perhaps they were attracted by the prospect of having "entire charge" of the school as described in the board's advertisement.

Four of them were chosen to come for interview, and the School Board assessed them by having each of them teach a class at the village school in their presence. The candidates were Miss Helen Steele of Ardlussa School on the Isle of Jura, Miss Ann Bell of Lundin Links in Fife, Miss Margaret Ewing of Paisley and Miss E Jack of Milton.

The weather was bad on the day of the interview and Helen Steele sent a rather dramatic telegram to the board:

CANNOT COME ON THURSDAY. SEA STORMY. NO BOAT DARE CROSS TO CRINAN. REGRET THIS VERY MUCH. LETTER BY POST

9: Annie Craig Bell: 1884 to 1905

The telegraph was the usual means of rapid communication at this time, though the telephone was just starting to become generally available. It was in the previous year that the School Board had given permission for a telegraph pole to be erected on ground owned by the school, so it was probable that the village had only recently been connected to the telegraph system.

Meanwhile the board voted on the remaining candidates, giving three votes each to Miss Jack and Miss Bell. The ability to reach a compromise was not one of their strong points, so they decided to put off making a decision and wait for Miss Steele to put in an appearance. She appeared and taught a class in front of the board a few days later, after the storm had subsided. The board voted again and this time gave four votes to Miss Bell and three to Miss Steele, so Miss Steele had to go back to her school on Jura disappointed, presumably undertaking the long journey by steamer from Greenock. One hopes she was a good sailor and could enjoy the beautiful scenery as she sailed past the Isle of Bute, along Loch Fyne, through the Crinan Canal and across the Sound of Jura to Ardlussa. At least she was travelling at the expense of the School Board.

Just what happened to Stewart Archibald and his family is not known. He does not appear to have found a new job by the beginning of the following year. The board tried to help him by giving him a certificate which expressed a favourable opinion of his ability and hoped he would soon be successful in getting a new appointment, explaining that *"on account of a decrease in population it seemed to the board desirable to appoint a female teacher"*. Presumably any potential employer would understand their logic of replacing a male teacher with a female teacher at a reduced salary in circumstances where the school roll had decreased, but today's Equal Opportunities Commission might be less understanding!

Although Annie Craig Bell had previously been teaching in the county of Fife on the other side of the country, she was born in Kilbirnie, not far away in Ayrshire. Her parents were Margaret and James, a gamekeeper, and she had a sister and a brother, William. She was 32 years old when she came to the parish to begin teaching at Side on December 1st. She is the first teacher at Side for whom we have a photograph, and about whom a verbal account has been passed down, so that for the first time we can get a clearer idea of what kind of person the Side teacher was.

The Side School

She seemed to be well liked by almost everyone. Elizabeth Crawford who started at the school in 1894 at the age of four talked to her daughter many years later about her school days, describing Miss Bell as a "wonderful person". Reports from her Majesty's Inspectors describe her as energetic on more than one occasion. They also comment on the good class discipline, though throughout her career there were never any reports of excessive punishment- or for that matter punishment of any kind, though no doubt she had the use of a tawse like all the teachers at that time. This together with the strong chin in the school photograph of 1894 suggests that she was anything but a timid or prim Victorian maid, and was more probably a rather determined but likeable young woman.

Her sister married a Mr. Congleton, and when their children Robert, Annie and William reached school age, they moved into the schoolhouse to live with their aunt and be educated at the school. Soon after taking up her post, Annie Bell's parents felt able to retire, and they also moved into the schoolhouse. And as if it was not crowded enough with the six if them in the little two up, two down schoolhouse, she also had a little black and white terrier dog to keep her company, occupying a central position in the school photograph of 1894. There are at least two other dogs in subsequent school photographs belonging to the teacher: they were obviously popular with Side school mistresses. Life in that crowded household must have been very different to that of the solitary bachelor existence of some of Annie Bell's predecessors.

Annie Bell got on well with the School Board. Unlike Stewart Archibald she did not pester them with letters complaining about deficiencies of the school house, but got on quietly and efficiently with her work, restoring the reputation of the school that had reached a low ebb under her predecessor. Her salary was a modest £50, and she got an additional £10 for supplying coals, cleaning the schoolhouse and supplying slates, pens, ink, chalk and towels for the school. She got small salary increases from time to time and was earning £65 by 1891, but even after 21 years service her salary was nowhere near that of her male predecessor.

In 1885 a new School Board was elected. The outgoing board held a public meeting as usual to give an account of their work of the previous three years. Although they had not felt able to give an honest explanation to Stewart Archibald of the reason for his dismissal, they were in no way ashamed of their action, and in the public meeting they bragged about their clever action which had the result that *"the work was done better for half the money"*

For the first (and only) time the Rev. James Murray was elected chairman in place of Mr. Peile, there having been some feeling against a having a chairman who did not reside in the parish. Mr. Peile lived at Inverkip House (now a nursing home) in Inverkip, not far from Ardgowan, the main residence of his employer, Sir Michael Shaw-Stewart. There was no love lost between the Rev James Murray and Mr. Peile. At the first board meeting, which was reported in detail in the Greenock Telegraph, there was a squabble about a proposal to change the starting time of board meetings to 8 pm in the evening. Mr. Peile protested that there was no train at that hour to get him back to his home in Inverkip, and he *"thought they ought to show some Christian charity in the matter for they knew he represented the interests of Sir Michael in the parish - who paid a large amount in rates - and these interests ought to be fully represented on the board"*. The Rev Murray's rather uncharitable response was that " *they recognised no interests at that board but the interest of education"*. The matter was resolved by farmer Thomson, who pointed out that though that late hour might suit the Glasgow people, his bedtime was at 8 pm because he had to rise at five in the morning.

They could ill afford to spend time on petty squabbles since they had a good deal of work on their hands. They were involved in a long standing dispute with their neighbouring School Board at Port Glasgow, who were unhappy about the fact that many children living on the edge of the parish of Kilmacolm found it more convenient to attend the Port Glasgow school. Not unnaturally the Port Glasgow board thought it unfair that their parish rate should be used to pay for the education of children from another parish, and there was much negotiation before an amount of financial compensation was agreed between the two School Boards. In addition to this, the village school at Kilmacolm, built originally in 1858 and subsequently extended on two occasions was proving to be too small for the needs of the parish. It was not feasible to make any more extensions so they decided to rebuild. The new school that was opened in 1887 was a handsome two story building catering for 600 children. As well as having conventional fireplaces it had an additional

The Side School

novel method of heating using hot water pipes.

The Rev Murray's colleagues were apparently not impressed by his performance as chairman of the board. After completing his term of office as chairman, both he and Mr. Peile were re-elected for a new term. At the first meeting of the new board in 1888 the Rev Murray was proposed for re-election as chairman, but an amendment in favour of Mr. Peile was passed, the instigator of the amendment commenting that he *"couldn't sit on the board with any satisfaction in view of Murray's conduct while chairman of the late board"*.

However, James Murray did get the satisfaction in the following year of seeing the abolition of all school fees in the parish, largely as a result of his own efforts.

Meanwhile Annie Bell had no difficulty in obtaining good reports from Her Majesty's Inspectors. Their first report on her class in 1885 stated:

> *The new teacher conducts the school with energy and intelligence and in respect of both discipline and instruction it is in a very creditable condition*

By 1887 the class numbers were increasing, possibly because some of the pupils who had transferred to the village school in Mr. Archibald's time came back to Side:

> *"The number presented for examination is considerably larger than usual. The best results again are found in the junior classes the older scholars being comparatively slow and backward. The classes in History and Geography make a rather better appearance this year but the subjects are not yet sufficiently known to merit a grant. More intelligence might be shown in the oral examination. Singing is spirited and tuneful. There is again a good display of industrial work. The discipline is good but simultaneous answering must be checked"*

The inspector's complaint about discipline makes rather depressing reading. The lively children knew the answer to the inspector's questions, and were not able to stop themselves calling out the answer. Such spontaneity had to be drilled out of them.

And in 1891:

> *"This continues to be a good specimen of a small country school ... very creditable to Miss Bell's*

skill and industry..."

The range of subjects being taught to the children was expanding a little during this period, to include for example music, drawing and *"nature knowledge"*. Singing had always been taught and was considered important enough for the class to perform before HM Inspectors, who commented on their performance in their report on the school. They were taught music theory through the tonic sol fah notation, and at one time a music teacher paid a weekly visit to Side to teach them. Various kinds of drawing were taught, described as freehand, geometry, perspective, model and map drawing. This subject was originally considered suitable only for boys, but by 1891 was also being taught to the girls. For *"nature knowledge"* they once had a visiting lecturer as Miss Bell reported in her log:

> *"Today Mr. Buchanan delivered his very interesting lecture: 'Nature Knowledge- Trees and their Story, illustrated by numerous specimens of their leaves'"*

At the village school they always had better facilities and a wider range of subjects than at Side. In a public meeting in 1891 Mr. Peile reported on behalf of the board:

> *"The Rev. Mr. Gregory was kind enough to volunteer to teach a short-hand class in the evenings of last winter, and his services were gladly accepted, and the minutes of 9th December 1890 record the board's sense of his kindness in undertaking work which proves of so much advantage to boys and young men who may enter offices. This class had very satisfactorily been taken advantage of, the number on the roll being 30"*

Shorthand was seen as a subject suitable only for boys, presumably because clerks and writers were always considered jobs for men. This situation changed when the use of the typewriter became commonplace, at which time this kind of work was considered suitable for women.

---

right: The Westside Public School in 1894.
back row, left to right: Mrs Huie, Annie Bell
second row: Peggy Crawford, Annie Crawford, unknown, unknown, Agnes Ross, Willie Orr
second row: Rachel Laird, unknown, Elizabeth Crawford, Maggie Peake, Polly Laird, unknown, unknown
front row: Willie Crawford, James Laird, Alec Laird, unknown, Bobby Baxter

The Side School

The School Board had another subject for study when in 1894 they set up a "Committee on Manners", which after deliberation reported that:

> *"teachers should be recommended in the course of their regular instruction to call the attention of scholars to the subject of manners, morals and temperance. It was further agreed that a few text books on these subjects should be provided for the teachers"*

Uppermost in the board's mind was probably the easy availability of alcohol, which had proved to be a great temptation to many people as an easy recourse to the hardships of the time. The temperance movement had started some years earlier in Scotland as a response to the scenes of depravity and widespread crime that occurred every Saturday night in Glasgow, which to many seemed to threaten the fabric of society. Annie Bell was secretary of the local Band of Hope and was responsible for countersigning the certificates or pledges through which people promised to abstain from all intoxicating liquors. We know that one of the children, Maggie (Peggy) Crawford signed the pledge in 1898 when she would have been about 11 or 12 years old. Presumably the idea was to catch people at an early age before they had time to get a taste for alcohol. Anne Bell was no doubt encouraged to use her influence to get all the children in her charge to sign the pledge.

Temptation was not far away. According to Kilmacolm resident Brownie McMinn, born circa 1885, a pile of stones close to Chapel farm marks the place where the Turf Inn stood, only a few hundred yards from the Side school:

> *"I have been told that most of the strong waters sold in that Inn were distilled in the Blackwater Glen, and never made the acquaintance of the revenue authorities".*

In the 1890s Bessie Lang and her sister Agnes started as pupils at the school. They lived at Midtown, now a ruin, on the road to Dippany and about a mile from the school. Elizabeth Crawford (Peggy Crawford's sister) used to pass Midtown on her way to school, and when the weather was bad, Bessie Lang would wrap her in her cloak to protect her from the weather. Bessie Lang was to have a long association with the village schools. After completing her education at Side, she gained her teaching certificate and became an assistant teacher at

BAND OF HOPE.

This is to Certify that **Maggie Crawford** is a MEMBER of the above Society having signed the following

PLEDGE

I promise by Divine Assistance to abstain from all INTOXICATING LIQUORS as beverages and to discountenance all the causes and practices of Intemperance.

Signed 23rd Ja 1898

_____ Secretary.

Side. Later on she transferred to the village school to teach there.

***

And so life at Side went on as the Victorian age progressed. In 1888 the Cutty Sark, built in Dumbarton across the Clyde, established a record passage of 71 days from Sydney to London. Towards the close of the century the Greenock Telegraph kept its readers enthralled with reports such as *"Towards the North Pole"*, complete with an artist's impression of a ship locked in an ice field. In 1897, Dr. Nansen, the famous Norwegian explorer lectured to an appreciative audience of 3000 in the Greenock Town Hall about his attempts to reach the North Pole.

British influence abroad was considerable. In 1897 the *Greenock Telegraph* reported a boundary dispute between Chile and Argentina. How to resolve the dispute? The *Greenock Telegraph* had the answer: refer the matter to Queen Victoria for arbitration!

1897 was also the year of the Queens Jubilee. Kilmacolm celebrated the event on June 22 in a big way, as the *Greenock Telegraph* reported:

The Side School

Wednesday, June 23, 1897   **The Greenock Telegraph and Clyde Shipping Gazette**

"Like all loyal subjects of Queen Victoria, the inhabitants of Kilmacolm observed a general holiday and closed all their business premises and shops during the day. The decorating of the housetops with flags and bunting was not forgotten and a creditable display was made. At ten o'clock in the forenoon the celebrations commenced, but the weather at that hour was far from inviting, rain falling heavily. The children of the parish assembled in the Public School playground and marched to the parish church. There a commemorative service was held and was conducted by the three ministers of the village, Revs. James Murray, James Fyfe and Thomas Gregory. At the close the National Anthem was sung. Marshalled again on the playground, the children each received a Jubilee medal. A procession was then formed and the large company proceeded by Ducal Avenue to a field on the estate, the use of which was kindly granted for the day by Sir Michael Shaw-Stewart. Refreshments having been served, a well arranged programme of sports was commenced. For the school children there were no less than twenty six items and these were all keenly contested. Fifteen items formed the adult portion of the program open to competition, all of which proved of an interesting nature. The "pic-nic" had also the attractions of dancing, cricket and football. The weather improved in the afternoon and everything passed off most successfully. In the evening an open air concert was given by "the village choir" under the leadership of Mr. J F Semple in the public park, where favourite Scottish songs were fairly well rendered. The concert opened with the singing of "God Save the Queen" and finished with "Auld Lang Syne". Shortly after nine o'clock a match was put to the large bonfire at the Laird's quarry. The fine blaze was the centre of attraction until the fireworks were let off in the grounds of Shalot, the residence of Mr. Adam Birkmyre. Many of the householders had their windows beautifully illuminated, and Mr. F McIlwraith had a star comprising eighty banners displayed from his housetop. The day's celebrations passed off without a hitch. Several excursion parties spent the day in the village, amongst them being the members and friends of Greenock Mount Park Free Church Sabbath School and a large contingent of boys from the Quarrier's Homes"

9: Annie Craig Bell: 1884 to 1905

The Side School

Improvements in medicine continued but even in a relatively healthy environment such as Kilmacolm there were frequent epidemics such as scarlet fever and diphtheria that closed the school down from time to time. They were life threatening diseases as evidenced by Annie Bell's log entry in 1893:

> *"have the painful duty of recording the death of Willie Orr of Newton who died today of scarlet fever"*

As the century drew to a close, many of the figures associated with the school passed away.

In October 1898 the Rev James Eckford Fyfe died at the age of 55, having been associated with the school both as chairman of the management committee of the Side subscription school prior to 1874, and serving for a total of fifteen years as a member of the Kilmacolm School Board. The Rev Thomas Gregory MA, Free Church minister took his place on the board.

It was the end of an era at the village school, when the head teacher Donald MacDonald retired in 1898. Ten years previously the board had suggested to him that he might like to retire, but he had declined. In 1898, when Mr. MacDonald had reached the age of 73 and had been teaching at the school for 42 years, the board decided that his time really had come, and informed Mr. MacDonald that he must retire. He was offered a generous pension of £200, or £160 if he wished to continue to live rent-free in the schoolhouse. He chose the latter, but he enjoyed only a short retirement before his death in 1900.

Mr. W L Walker, Donald MacDonald's assistant, took over as head teacher at the village school. Only a month after his appointment, Mr. Walker was faced with an extraordinary situation when eight or nine hundred children were marched through the village to the village school, headed by Mr. William Quarrier who demanded that they should be educated there.

This was the culmination of a long dispute between the School Board and William Quarrier, who had founded the nearby Quarrier's Orphan Homes. The orphans came from all parts of Scotland, but the orphan homes were in the parish of Kilmacolm, and when the parochial council charged the Homes an education rate Mr.

---

left: Queen Victoria's Jubilee celebrations in Kilmacolm in 1897

Quarrier reasoned that the village school ought to be responsible for educating the children. There was a lively public meeting of the outgoing School Board at which Mr. Quarrier was present, and a good deal of argument between Mr. Quarrier and the School Board, represented by Mr. Peile and the Rev Murray and for once in agreement. Having failed to persuade the School Board, Quarrier tried unsuccessfully to get himself elected on the new board, and on the day of the election he had a number of the orphan children parade the streets with bills saying "*Vote for Quarrier and the Orphans*". Later on he brought a court case against the board but was again unsuccessful.

In 1900 the Boer war was in progress. Nigel MacMillan, now aged 55 and living in Dumfriesshire found the time to record many of his thoughts in poetry, and as the last few stanzas of his poem show, he was dissatisfied with the conduct of this war:

It is not a war of honour
But a war of shame and lies
A disgrace to the British nation
Before the world's eyes

I do not blame our soldiers
Their duty is to fight
Theirs not to question
Be the quarrel wrong or right

But I blame the Caitiff traitors
High in offices of state
To gratify whose greed of gold
Homes are made desolate

In 1901, the longest reign in British history ended with the death of the Queen. For some years afterwards her reign was remembered when the school closed for two days in May for Victoria Day. They got an additional day off in May 1903 when her son Bertie, now King Edward, visited Glasgow.

The School Board continued to adjudicate on requests for use of the school facilities outside of school hours.

---

right: Donald MacDonald, head teacher of the Kilmacolm Public School, and his successor William Walker c 1889

The Side School

9: Annie Craig Bell: 1884 to 1905

The Side School

In 1903 they decided that the dancing lessons being held at the village school were *"not conducive to public morality"* and they were discontinued. Subsequently there was a request to hold dancing lessons at Side, but this was also turned down. For some reason they also discontinued the use of Side for religious meetings on Sundays, permission for which had been granted to a local farmer since 1885 on behalf of a *"religious body known as the Plymouth Brethren"*. They showed more flexibility in dealing with the children however when they gave permission to children who lived more than two miles away to leave at 3 pm in the winter months, thus allowing them to make their journey home in daylight.

The question of punishment was also reviewed by the board, probably in response to complaints from parents in the village, and an education subcommittee decided to *"recommend to the teachers to discontinue corporeal punishment for inefficiency in lessons"*. They had realised in other words that it was not possible to beat instruction into the children, but they did not feel strongly enough to make more than a *recommendation* to the teachers.

The Inspectors report for Side in 1903 was good as usual, but there was sting in the tail:

" ... methods of teaching are somewhat non-modern. Certain points worthy of attention have been brought to the notice of the teacher"

By this time Annie Bell had lost much of the energy that the school inspectors had observed when she started teaching at Side. She had suffered a long illness in 1892 which had prevented her from teaching for eight months. The School Board were sympathetic and had engaged a temporary teacher, Miss Agnes MacDonald, keeping Miss Bells job open for her until she recovered. The Rev. Fyfe visited her and reported her progress to the board, and Miss Bell *"returned her best thanks to the board for their kindness and co-operation"*.

left: Westside Public School c.1900
back row left to right: Willie Carson, Archie Duff, Bobby Baxter, Johnny Baxter
second row: Alex Laird, Mary Paton, Rachael Laird, Margaret Ross, Johnny Carson,
front row: Jenny Andrew, Agnes Lang, Bessie Lang, Mary Crawford, Peggy Duff, Jenny Crawford, Katie Andrew, Lizzie Crawford

Annie Bell's mother had died in 1897, and in 1904 she closed the school on account of her father's illness. He died later that year. Annie herself became ill soon afterwards, and as on the previous occasion, the board gave her leave of absence and engaged a temporary teacher. But Annie's illness got worse and in May 1905 at the age of 53 she felt she had to resign. The board gave her a pension of £20 and she got an equal amount from the Scotch Education department, so she was left to live on the miserable sum of £40, a quarter the pension that Donald MacDonald got, and without the option that he had of continuing to live in the schoolhouse. In the event, the amount was somewhat academic, because Annie died less than a year later. The Side school closed for half a day on the occasion of her funeral, and Annie was buried in the cemetery in Kilmacolm alongside her mother and father.

The *Greenock Telegraph* report read:

> "General regret was felt in Kilmacolm on Saturday when the news became generally known that Miss Annie C Bell, the late mistress of the West Side school had passed away. Appointed over 20 years ago, Miss Bell laboured patiently and conscientiously and was a great favourite with scholars, *parents and School Board, and her work always received the favourable commendation of HM Inspector. Miss Bells genial presence and kindly smile will be greatly missed in the district in which she was so well known."*

There must have been hundreds like her: quiet, hard-working Victorian women, paid barely enough to live on and with very few alternative jobs open to them. There was enough money to give her a Christian burial, but none for a tombstone. Her grave in the cemetery at Kilmacolm is unmarked.

Chapter Ten
Mabel Maclaren
1905 to 1930

Following Annie Bell's resignation, the School Board appointed Miss Mabel Elizabeth Maclaren to take over at Side. She was to be the longest serving teacher at Side, seeing the school through the periods of the Great War and the Depression, as well as through administrative changes when the parish-based School Board system became a county-based Education Authority.

Mabel had a reputation for being strict, and when a young girl like Isobel MacDonald started at the school in about 1918 she confessed to being terrified of her teacher. This was not primarily because of her teacher's strictness however, but because Mabel was black, and Isobel had never seen a black person before. Mabel's father, Alexander Maclaren, was a black engineer from Greenock, and her mother Mary Ann was white. There were probably people of many races in a town like Greenock where the seafaring folk travelled the world, but black people would have been uncommon in the relatively isolated countryside round Kilmacolm. While the younger children were frightened of her, the older boys, inevitably perhaps, behaved in the cruel manner of boys of that age by referring to her as the "auld nigger".

In the conservative times at the start of the twentieth

century, Mabel would certainly have found her colour a handicap in integrating into the community round Side. She did make friends however with the Orr brothers, Robert and William, just across the road from the school at Gateside farm. They were both well read and the brothers often entertained Mabel in the evenings, the three of them enjoying long conversations until late into the night. Mabel fell in love with one of the brothers, but her feelings were not returned, reinforcing her sense of isolation in the schoolhouse.

If the children were fearful of Miss Maclaren, she clearly thought a lot of them. She wanted the children to look their best in school photographs, so she kept a private supply of the elaborate collars that were fashionable then for the girls who she considered needed improvement. And when there was a complaint from Miss Love[1] of Margaret's Mill farm about the children damaging the dry stone walls bounding the school property, Mabel was quick to rush to the defence of the children. She pointed out that the walls were in a tumble-down condition, and anyway it was the horses belonging to the Loves that did the damage. The children being from farming families would know better than to damage fences in this way. The School Board of course went along with this and denied all responsibility.

Mabel was also clearly delighted when two of her pupils - Jeannie Scott and Mary Black - won prizes in the industrial sections of the Renfrewshire show in Paisley in 1923. Jean Hepburn won again in 1924. Her exhibit was a pair of knitted stockings which won her a second prize certificate and a cash prize of 7/6 (38p). Mabel was so pleased that she gave Jean an additional prize, a small wooden box, as a personal present from her.

Soon after Mabel's appointment at Side, there was an election for a new School Board and a proposal was made that a woman should stand for the board. The reporter for the Greenock Telegraph was clearly unsure whether such an extraordinary proposal should be taken seriously, reporting:

---

[1] Miss Love was a descendant of Jock Love, who featured 50 or more years earlier in the history of the school as a pupil at the old subscription school.

---

right: a fragment of a letter from Mabel Maclaren to the School Board about a complaint against the children

The Side School

Westside School.
Kilmacolm.
30th Oct. 1912

J. Cleghorn Hair Esq.
Royal Bank.

Dear Sir,
Yours to hand of 29th inst. Regarding the complaint of the children breaking down the fences & dykes on Margaret's mill f[arm] I may say that the children are not to blame [as th]e fences and dykes are in [a] tumble down condition, [as] may easily be seen, [but] by Mr. Love complained that the children [had] broken down a d[yke] to go near their fields.

I remain,
Yrs. faithfully
Mabel E. McLaren.

10: Mabel Maclaren: 1905 to 1930

The Side School

> *"In some quarters the proposal made by the Rev T Gregory that an endeavour should be made to get a lady on the board is taken seriously"*

Women had always been eligible as board members, and it was not at all uncommon for women to sit on School Boards throughout the country, but it took some time for a revolutionary idea like this to reach Kilmacolm. When Mrs. Isabel Reid Barr, referred to as the *"wife of Mr. R L Barr, a technical chemist"* stood as a candidate, she attracted a good deal of attention in the election. In the pre-election public meeting over 100 turned up including several ladies. When the male candidates addressed the audience, they were at their most patronising, suggesting that a *"Star of Venus was going to rise on the educational horizon"*. One of them suggested that the only reason for the lady's candidature was *"because the law allows it"*, later conceding that *"the lady might be a good member and he was not hostile towards her"*. In the end Isabel Barr was successful in her campaign. She and Dr. Peter Alexander Laird, a surgeon from Kilmacolm who like Isabel Barr was sitting on the board for the first time, formed a subcommittee that represented the Side school. She visited Side in June 1906 and wrote in the log:

> *"visited the school today. Heard one class read very well also heard the singing which was good.."*

The question of prizes for the children was a matter that occupied the School Board. They had always given prizes for attendance, but there was a feeling that they should now award merit prizes. This came to a head in 1909 when Dr. Laird decided to take up the issue. The *Greenock Telegraph* recorded what happened.

> *'Breezy "Scene" at School Board Meeting: Member Leaves the Meeting: Dr. Laird proposed reducing the number of attendance prizes and increase the number of merit prizes...."*

It was not the first time he had brought up the matter, and although he got some support, the motion was defeated. There was a squabble, personal remarks were made and Dr. Laird walked out of the meeting, refusing to stand for another term of office at the forthcoming board election. It was typical of the board at its worst,

---

left: The Westside Public School in 1905
On Mabel Maclaren's left is Bessie Lang, Robert Lang and Mary Crawford. Agnes Lang is on Mabel Maclaren's right, next to the end of the row. Willie Crawford is in front of Bessie Lang.

seemingly unable to resist petty squabbles of this sort. In spite of the board's decision, later that year they decided to give two merit prizes in each subject in addition to attendance prizes. But the importance of attendance prevailed, and even in 1919 the Education Authority Attendance Committee ruled that a silver watch should be awarded for seven years perfect attendance and a gold medallion for nine years perfect attendance. Annie Fergusson a Side pupil who stayed at Hardridge farm was one of the first to claim a prize from the Education Authority, getting a silver watch in 1919.

The new board discovered that they could claim £40 from the Scottish Education Department if they employed an ex-pupil teacher as an assistant, and in January 1907 they appointed Miss Sarah Wylie from Clune Park to teach at Side. Mabel must have been delighted to get an assistant to help her, with 40 children to teach with ages varying between 5 and 13, not to mention the administration of the school as a whole. From then on Mabel Maclaren was always proud to be known as the *head mistress* of the Side school.

```
.. Kilmacolm School Board ..

        WEST-SIDE
    PUBLIC SCHOOL.

Class ..... VI .....

        .. PRIZE ..
            FOR

    Diligence and Progress

        AWARDED TO
        Agnes G Lang

            MABEL M'LAREN.
                Head Mistress.
Session 190
```

The Side School

Sarah Wylie stayed for only 9 months before she resigned. Between 1907 and 1917 a succession of assistant teachers - Sarah Farrell, Ann MacKinlay, Grace Kennedy and Flora McKinnon - were employed for short periods. The assistant teachers lived in with Mabel Maclaren at the schoolhouse, and there is a suspicion that the reason for the rapid turnover in staff was that Mabel was not the easiest person either to live with or to work with.

In 1910 Halley's Comet made its regular appearance. Nigel MacMillan could not resist putting pen to paper to record the event:

Why did we fear that death was near
Why did we take alarm
The comet went waltzing past our sphere
With his tail thrown over his arm

He chucked the old moon under the chin
He winked to Venus and to Mars
But he did not find the ladies in
When he called for the Seven Stars

Old Mother Earth with a knowing leer
Invited a whisk from his tail
But he knew quite well that her atmosphere
Was as good as a coat of mail

The comet was not to be caught with chaff
His tail might come to harm
So he gathered it up with a merry laugh
And carried it over his arm

He does not court Celestial Strife
Nor threaten with fire and hail
He leads a sober single life
And takes good care of his tail

Happy and gay he waltzed away
Among the rolling spheres
We'll have him back on the same old trace
In seventy seven years

In 1917 Elizabeth (Bessie) Lang, an ex-pupil of Side was appointed as assistant teacher, and she stayed on at Side until 1925. At this time the number of pupils at Side had decreased from over 40 in 1917 to about 18 in

10: Mabel Maclaren: 1905 to 1930

1925, and because of this decrease in roll Bessie Lang was transferred to the village school. Unlike the other assistant teachers, Bessie Lang did not stay in the schoolhouse. She lived with her mother and sister Agnes just half a mile from the school at Mountblow. She had a pony which she would sometimes lead to the school to graze to keep the grass down in the garden and playground.

Bessie Lang inherited a strict system of discipline from Mabel Maclaren which mellowed in later years as she moved away from Side and Mabel's influence. She was always well liked by both pupils and teachers. She and her sister are remembered in the village as an active couple who "*ran everywhere*". She came back to teach at Side from time to time whenever the teacher there was ill, and lived to a good age, still teaching in the village school in the 1950's.

Salaries for teachers were by this time increasing a little. By 1912 Mabel was earning £75 p.a. and this had increased to £125 (plus her rent-free accommodation in the school house) in 1918. At this time Bessie Lang got £100, while Mr. Walker, the head teacher in the village school got £350.

As always the School Board were very much involved with the welfare of the children, and they did not confine themselves to just educational matters. In 1910 Mr. W L Walker, the head teacher of the village school, informed the board that the children's' work was suffering because of the amount of farm work they had to carry out before and after school, and he asked if they could do anything about it. Even very young children had to work, sometimes as much as 40 hours per week in addition to their school work. One might have expected that the School Board would be tempted to look for another authority to take responsibility for such a request, but in 1910 the School Board had no doubt that this was within their province. They set up a working party and established a set of bylaws to control the employment of children, both in term time and during the holidays. Whether these bye laws - which presumably carried no legal force whatever - solved the problem or not is not recorded, but one has to admire the board for caring and their willingness to get involved.

The board were preoccupied with the benefits of fresh air, in accordance with the common belief of the time that most diseases were transmitted through the air,

The Side School

and had installed a new system of ventilation at Side using air trunking ducts in the roof space. It is a pity that they never attached the same importance to the provision of a reliable and clean water supply, the unreliable water supply at Side probably being responsible for a good deal of illness among the children.

The board were however concerned about the use of slates, and banned their use in favour of jotters except in the infant classes. Their concern with slates was the boys' habit of first spitting on them before wiping them clean, with the risk of spreading disease.

In 1912 it came to the notice of the School Board that there were goings on in the ice cream shops in Kilmacolm. There was suspicion that games of chance were taking place. It was one of those situations that gives credence to a belief in the more innocent times of the past, when people's concern about the behaviour of their children was not with drugs, sex and violence, but with card games and vanilla ice cream. On this occasion the board did not feel it had direct jurisdiction over the ice cream shop, and they merely recommended to the County Council that the shop should be made to close at 10.00 pm.

By now, the memory of Queen Victoria was starting to fade a little. In 1907 the school was closed for the usual two day holiday in May to celebrate Victoria day, but by 1909 the same holiday was called Empire day. In 1911 the board decided not to celebrate Empire day because there was already an additional national holiday to celebrate the coronation of King George V following the sudden death of Victoria's son, Edward VII, in the previous year.

The school started to get a few more facilities and equipment for the children. The board allocated £5 to start a small library at the school. Mr. James Coates gifted more books to the library in 1911 and Mrs. Huie contributed more in 1914. The school also got a piano that was surplus to requirements at the village school, new maps of Europe and Africa (no doubt updated to show the progress of the Empire), a sewing machine, a new clock, and a weighing machine.

Mrs. Huie, who gifted books to the Side library, was the wife of J Cleghorn Huie of the Royal Bank in Kilmacolm and treasurer of the School Board. The Huies were associated with the school over a period of over thirty years. Mrs. Huie appeared in a number of the school photographs and frequently visited the school, especially at Christmas when he gave the children their Christmas treat. Even when the family moved to Edinburgh, the couple found time to visit the school on their return visits to the village.

The Shaw-Stewarts also continued to visit the school. The teachers log book records a visit in 1907 from Lady Alice who had succeeded Lady Octavia:

> *Lady Alice gave the children their Christmas treat and the children were dismissed a little earlier*

But the end of an era was approaching. The Great War came in 1914, affecting the lives of everyone, even in this remote school. After the war nothing would be quite the same again: the patronage of the gentry would end, and the School Board system would be replaced.

In 1914, a Mr. Bain presented the school with a war map, so that the children could be informed of the progress of the war. The expectation was probably that the children would be able to follow on the map the advances and eventual victory of the British forces against the aggressors. The reality of the stalemate in the trenches was not at all what was expected.

At first the war seemed rather remote and unimportant to the children. There was a minor disappointment when at the end of the school year in 1914 the board decided not to award any prizes. Then they lost the services of their singing teacher when he was called up for National Service, and of their physical training teacher because the train service had become uncertain. However the reality of the war was brought home to them in a much more personal way in April 1915 when Miss Maclaren recorded in her log:

> *"It is with the deepest regret that we record the death (from wounds received in France) of Archie Duff, Dykefoot Farm, a former pupil of this school"*

And again in 1916:

> *"James Sands has been killed in France"*

Archie Duff appears in the school photograph of 1900. He served as a private with the Seaforth Highlanders. James Sands was mentioned in the school log when he and Bessie Lang won prizes for recitation and singing seven years earlier in 1908. There were almost certainly other casualties, though two deaths out of a class with about twenty boys is a high enough ratio.

It might be assumed that farmers were exempt from

The Side School

war service, but in the Great War many of the farmers and farm workers went to fight. When Mabel's assistant teacher resigned in 1917, Mabel recorded in her log:

> *"Have communicated with the board regarding the decrease in roll and that as several families have removed from the district and the houses are likely to be untenanted until after the war there will be little increase for some time. The board have decided to postpone the appointment of an assistant in the meantime"*

There were so few farm workers left that they had to enlist the help of the children to lift the potato crop. With the approval of the School Board the children were released from school to gather the crop - a change from the usual circumstance where the Compulsory Officer was in conflict with the parents to get the children off the land and into school. The exercise was co-ordinated by Mr. Walker, head teacher in the village school, and afterwards he reported back to the board on the success of the operation:

> *"The children were let out in squads of from 1 to 8 and no child was out for more than 10 days. They worked on 19 different farms and the money earned amounted to £82-12-3. The farmers expressed themselves as thoroughly satisfied with the work done and the behaviour of the children"*

The board also co-operated with the authorities by making the school facilities available to the local Food Economy Committee for practical demonstrations in economical cookery.

Eventually the war ended and the armistice was signed. The children observed two minutes silence, heard an address on the war, and sang "God Save the King", a practice that was continued in years to come. A War Bonus of £10 was granted to each teacher, £10 to the janitor and £5 to the assistant janitor, and they were awarded a 3 day special peace holiday in 1919. The board noted that during the war, 1079 free books had been supplied to necessitous cases in the parish, including fatherless children and children of parents on active service

In 1919, the system under which the provision of education in the parish was managed by a School Board ended. Mr. Peile, who had served on the board as chairman practically since its inception, had died in

10: Mabel Maclaren: 1905 to 1930

1916. His old sparring partner, the Rev James Murray, paid tribute to his "*shrewd and practical wisdom*" and his more than 40 years of faithful service.

At the final board meeting in May 1919:

> "*Mr. Murray favoured the meeting with a most interesting account of the progress of education in Scotland since the 18th century with one or two interesting episodes in the history of the Kilmacolm board.*"

For all their faults, the School Board had served the community well over their 47 year history. They were made up of a reasonably representative cross section of the community, typically consisting of two farmers, two ministers, and two business men, lead by Mr. Peile as chairman representing the interests of the Lord Lieutenant of the County. Looking back we would observe that there was hardly any female representation, and there was still a kind of feudal element in the strong influence that the Lord Lieutenant of the county could exert through his factor, Mr. Peile. But on the whole the board were practical men with the interests of the children at heart, applying themselves effectively to meet the educational needs of the community.

The new Education Authority was a county organisation, and their first meeting was at County Hall in Paisley in April 1919. At first they were separate from the county council organisation, but in 1930 they became a department of the Local Government of the County. For the purposes of education the county was divided into five districts, each district having a School Management Committee to handle local issues, district 4 covering the two schools in Kilmacolm. The School Management Committees were staffed by teachers and parents as well as Education Authority members to give it some local representation, but their authority was very limited compared with that of the central authority. The authority established twelve standing committees to cover matters such as Attendance, Medical Inspection and Treatment, Religious and Temperance Instruction, Finance, Property and Supplies. They defined 17 items that needed urgent attention, including existing schemes for free books, summer holidays and special holidays for the King's birthday and the peace treaty, and prizes.

left: Robert Orr at Gateside farm c.1919, Side in the background

The Education Authority gave their attention to the salaries of men and women teachers. The Committee on Teaching set starting salaries for non-graduates to £100 for women and £110 for men. They met again only a week later and in an enlightened moment set identical starting salaries of £120 for both men and women. Six months later they thought better of it and adopted salary scales starting at £130 for women, and £150 for men.

The provision of medical treatment for the children had been gradually improving since the beginning of the century. Under the old School Board system they had the services of a County Medical Officer and a nurse, but under the new Education Authority, medical provisions were taken up on a more organised basis. In 1906 eyesight testing was carried out in the village school, initially by the teacher, and the short list of children with problems was seen by the doctor. Thirty three children were found to have significant sight problems. In some cases free spectacles were supplied. Dental examinations started in 1914, and free dental treatment was given to necessitous children. Schools were visited to check on the sanitary arrangements and to observe the children at physical drill, looking for cases of spinal curvature, eruptions or sores and poor nutrition. There was instruction in personal cleanliness and *"handkerchief drill"*.

The County Medical Officer was not at all satisfied about the unreliable water supply and the primitive toilet facilities at Side. The water supply at Side consisted of a chamber dug in the farmers field just up the hill from Side which for most of the time caught the water as it drained down the hill, but often became empty in dry seasons. Water was piped from the tank to the school where there was a hand pump. Unfortunately the chamber also caught any wildlife that might happen to fall in, not to mention any manure that the farmer had used on his field. The medical officer specified that water should be piped from the mains supply in the village, but this work was never carried out, probably for reasons of cost. Corrective work was limited to installing a galvanised iron cistern in the playground which stored rainwater collected from the roof as an additional water supply, and installing new dry closets.

The job of emptying the closets each week, the contents being tipped into a pit in the neighbouring field, fell to the assistant janitor. Side was not big enough to

The Side School

have its own janitor, and the janitor from the village and his assistant were responsible for Side as well as the village school. In 1929 the Education Authority advertised for a janitor for Kilmacolm to succeed the late James Noble. He had to be between 30 and 45 years old, married, and preferably an ex-serviceman. His wage was 47/6 (£2.38) per week plus 15/6 (£0.78) in lieu of house, light and fuel, and he got a pension after 15 years service. A uniform, dungarees and boots were supplied. Jimmy Whittet got the job, a man who was said to have been in the trenches at the age of 16, having lied about his age to be accepted by the army. His assistant was Bobby Crawford ("Old Bobbie"), who was disabled by gassing in the war.

The Education Authority were very particular about the appearance of the janitor, and when it was reported that certain janitors were presenting a slovenly appearance by wearing a mixture of uniform and plain clothes, they specified that the full uniform had to be worn during school hours, complete with dark buttons showing the county crest along with war service medals.

Another of the jobs of the janitor was to take the children in their drill class, both at the village school and at Side. Drill was a subject that had always been taken seriously, starting from the early days when Stewart Archibald in 1883 reported in his log:

> *"Have recommended giving scholars a little military drill twice a week on Tuesdays and Thursdays for 20-30 minutes"*

For a period, the School Board arranged for a drill sergeant from Greenock to visit the school to supervise drill, but by 1893 the janitor was giving lessons in what was described a musical drill. By 1908, the subject assumed an even greater importance when legislation was passed to ensure that all children were taught. The reason for this interest was that in the Boer war, eight thousand out of eleven thousand army recruits in Manchester were found to be unfit for military service. A specialist drill instructor visited the school and Mabel Maclaren reported that:

> *"we have this week received a number of bar bells for the use of older children in drill"*

By 1920 they were a little more relaxed about the whole thing, and Mabel supervised the boys - and girls - herself in physical exercise. Mabel lead by example. She carried a stick which she would hold vertically behind her back to demonstrate correct posture with a straight back.

It is possible to get first hand evidence of work and play in Mabel Maclaren's class from a number of her ex-pupils. At lunch time and play time their favourite game was Foxes and Hounds which they played up the hill behind the school among the rocks and bracken, a perfect play area, though not on school property. There was even a large smooth stone, always referred to as "*the sliding stone*" which was used as a natural slide.

The children had a special treat in 1920 when Mabel recorded

> "*Miss MacKay entertained the children to a cinematograph display*"

-probably the first time the children had seen moving pictures. And in 1921:

> "*Mrs. Huie has kindly gifted a gramophone*"

At lunch time, the children ate their "*piece*", usually bread and jam. The Education Authority had decreed that school lunches should be provided in all schools, and in December 1919 proudly announced that a "*hot meal at midday was being supplied in every part of the county*", but their decision was never implemented at Side. Mabel Maclaren made up for it to some extent by making the children hot cocoa at lunch time when the weather was cold.

The children's other play area was down by the burn, the Green Water, which is across the road from the school, no more than 200 metres away. Crossing the road, or even playing in it (as the children were clearly doing in the informal school photograph of circa 1919) was never regarded as hazardous, in view of the tiny amount of traffic. But all that changed in 1924 when Mabel had to record in her log:

> *21/3/24 "It is with the deepest regret that I record a distressing accident by which John Blair Lyle, our youngest scholar, has lost his life. A motor car was passing and the little child was knocked down by it. He succumbed to his injuries a few hours after in Greenock Infirmary".*

Afterwards the Education Authority expressed sympathy but accepted no liability. Caution signs were erected on either side of the school, and some time later the Chief Constable of Paisley visited the school and spoke to the children on "*Safety First*"

The Side School

The quality of roads had improved greatly by this time to accommodate the increasing use of motorised transport. In 1925 the first motor bus (called *"the Pioneer"*) ran between Port Glasgow and Kilmacolm. Also the compulsory officer, Mr. Swan, know to everyone as *"Old Swannie"* was able to use a bicycle to pay his weekly visit to the school to check for absentees.

The Education Authority also owned bicycles. In 1928 their executive officer reported that:

> *"a bicycle (already used) the property of the authority, has been overhauled and granted to Mr. Donald Bain, Dykefoot farm for use of his son Ian for the purpose of attending Greenock High School"*

Children who lived more than three miles from the school were entitled to transport to and from school at the expense of the Education Authority, and Mr. Donald Blain was paid 7/6 (37p) per day for taking his four children together with Wilhelmina and Agnes McLarty of Garshangen to and from the Side school in a horse-drawn vehicle. Soon afterwards this job was taken over by James C Anderson, carriage hirers of Kilmacolm, presumably in a motorised vehicle.

There was another advance in technology in 1929 when electric lighting was installed in the village school, though electricity was never provided at Side.

As usual progress was being made in increasing the range of subjects taught to the children. In 1913 a course of lessons in agriculture was given at Side. Mabel Maclaren suggested teaching butter making as a supplementary course for girls, which the board were happy to approve. However the distinction between Side and the village school where a much wider variety was available was well demonstrated when continuation classes were advertised at the village school in English, Geography, Arithmetic, Writing, Art, Needlework, Agriculture, Commercial Arithmetic, Cookery, Dressmaking, Drawing, Millinery, Needlework, Physical Culture, Hygiene and Laws of Health (for females), Shorthand and Woodwork. At Side the corresponding list of subjects consisted of just Plain Needlework!

They did their best to improvise wherever possible. The girls were taught cooking using the coal fired

108

10: Mabel Maclaren: 1905 to 1930

range in the kitchen in the teacher's house. Mabel made sure they cleaned it afterwards.

All the ex-pupils had their own view of discipline at the school under Mabel Maclaren. Mabel and Bessie each had their own strap. They were displayed, in a prominent position at the front of the class, hanging over the fireguard. Mabel's strap had one tail and Bessie's had several, and everyone agreed that they both used them liberally. But surprisingly although the children were in fear of their teachers, most of them respected or even liked them, seeing nothing untoward in their strict methods.

As an eleven year old in 1926 Jimmy Black was less willing than the younger children to accept the punishment freely meted out by Mabel on his fellow pupils, and he tells the story of how he took direct action by secretly taking her strap, cutting it up into small pieces with his penknife and dropping the pieces in the horse dung in the stables at his father's farm. Inevitably he was found out. Mabel, who could well predict the behaviour of his parents did not punish him herself, but gave him a note to take home. Jimmy's father knew the proper course of action to take. He bought a new strap for the school, and checked its effective operation on Jimmy, before having him deliver it into the hands of his adversary at the school.

The Hepburn sisters, Lizzie and Jean, recalled that two children from the Sailors and Orphan homes who went to the village school and got into some kind of trouble there, possibly shoplifting, were transferred to Side where Mabel soon got them under control. They also recalled that Mabel's technique for dealing with bad language was to take the offending child outside and

---

left: Westside Public School in 1919
back row, left to right: John Laird, James Lang, Adam Carson, Duncan McDougal, Bobby Harrild, Donald Black
fifth row: Marion Black, Annie Smith, Peggie Hepburn, Nan Fergusson, Mary Duff, Jenny Black, Mabel Maclaren, Willie Hepburn
fourth row: Bessie Lang, May Sim, May Scott, Jean Harrild, Kate Fergusson, Mary Smith, Jean Scott, Mary Black, Jenny Hankinson, John Black, James Todd
third row: Jean Carson, Jean Hepburn, Mary McGlynn, Jessie Fergusson, Maggie MacDonald, Lizzie Hepburn, Katie Harrild, Isobel MacDonald, Nettie Scott, Annie MacDonald, Hugh Blair
second row: Willie Black, Ian Sim, James Black, Pat McGlynn, James McGlynn, John Black, James McDougal
front row: Ian Smith, David Carson, John Smith

10: Mabel Maclaren: 1905 to 1930

wash out his or her mouth with carbolic soap.

Serious and persistent offenders were sent to the Industrial School in Greenock, and for offending children who had reached the age of twelve there was the Empress Training ship, where no doubt discipline was severe enough to give second thoughts to even the most recalcitrant youthful offender.

One of the highlights of the year for the school children was the annual Sabbath School trip. This event started in Annie Bell's time, but it was in the 1920s that it reached it's peak. It was quite an event, typical of the time. Somehow it is unimaginable that such an event could take place today. It was always held on the third Wednesday in June. Almost everyone went, leaving the village practically deserted. Each of the village churches had different destinations, but they shared the transport arrangements. They were piped onto their special excursion train at Kilmacolm Station bound for the Princes Pier in Greenock. There they boarded a special steamer which took them to their destinations in the islands and lochs of the Clyde, such as Port Bannatyne on the Isle of Bute, Largs in Ayrshire and Tighnabruaich on the Cowal Peninsula. All the children went, the schools being closed of course, accompanied by many of their parents. They children each took their *"tinnies"* (tin mugs) and milk for the little ones, the picnic being provided for them. The teachers and parents joined in as they played games and ran races.

The Sabbath School trip continued through the period of the General Strike in 1926 and through the depression in the early 1930s. The children were obviously aware of the General Strike: Mabel noted in her log

> *"The Strike has unsettled the children slightly in their attendance",*

---

left: Westside Public School in 1924
back row, left to right: Mabel Maclaren, Lawrence Todd, Willie Black, Lizzie Hepburn, Mrs Huie, John Black, James McDougal, Jean Hepburn, Bessie Lang
middle row: Peter McGlynn, Johnny Gemmell, Frank Blair, Sammy Goodwin, Malcolm Smith, Mary Buntin, Jimmy Todd, Mattie McCord, Polly Fergusson, Margaret Black, Jimmy Black, Katy Harrild, Tommy Carson
front row: David Buntin, Jimmy Black, Mary Black, Anna Black

It was in 1926 that Nigel MacMillan, pupil at the school in the 1850's gave his lecture on *"Old Times"* at the time of his retirement. Over the years he had become a respected member of the community, having been made a Justice of the Peace and elected as a Chieftain of the Clan MacMillan. Unfortunately he died only six weeks after delivering his lecture, and was not able to fulfil his intention of retiring to a house in Largs that he had purchased. On his tombstone over the MacMillan grave in Greenock is inscribed his verse:

> *"We hae our day and hae our say*
> *Then quit the scene for ithers*
> *And cuddle doon amang the mools*
> *Where mankind a' are brithers"*.

Nigel's school friend Jock Love had died 9 years earlier at Margarets Mill at the age of 74. During his lifetime he had farmed at Gateside and West Side, never moving more than a few hundred yards from the place of his birth, Margarets Mill where he spent the last years of his life. In spite of the amorous adventures of his youth he died a bachelor.

The school inspectors had no doubt about Mabel Maclaren's capability, and their reports were consistently good. For example, in 1926:

> *"This small school continues to be excellently managed. The children are intelligent and well informed and their advancement in the main subjects at the different stages is highly creditable to the teacher in charge. It is satisfactory to report that the teaching of cookery has been resumed"*

and in 1930:

> *"This little school continues to do most valuable work. The children are frank, intelligent and interested in their lessons and the teacher spares no pains in order that each pupil may advance as rapidly as his or her ability allows. It is noted with satisfaction that the pupil qualified for Advanced Division instruction is now conveyed to Kilmacolm Public School where facilities are much greater than can be afforded here"*

This was Mabel Maclaren's last school report. She was diabetic and had been unwell for the last few years. During the summer holidays of 1930 she and her sister Ada, who lived in Dunoon, had taken a holiday in

The Side School

Portnahaven on the island of Islay in the West Highlands where she died suddenly. She was 50 years old. The notice of her death in the Greenock Telegraph read:

> *"Kilmacolm has sustained a loss by the death of Miss Mabel Maclaren who had been headmistress of West Side school for a quarter of a century. Miss Maclaren was spending a holiday with relatives in Portnahaven, Islay when she died. Her health had not been too robust for several years but she declined to take a rest from her duties though the Education board were quite agreeable, preferring to devote herself to the task of educating the young and so practically died in harness. Miss Maclaren was a most successful teacher, being complimented for her work by parents, the School Board and HM Inspectors. She identified herself with everything connected with charitable and social work of the parish and did good service during the war."*

10: Mabel Maclaren: 1905 to 1930

Chapter Eleven
Elizabeth Browning
1930 to 1951

On May 17, 1930, the *Greenock Telegraph* carried a report of a lecture given by an American scientist called Professor Goddard. Professor Goddard made a prediction that must have been unbelievable to many, that it would be possible for man to travel to the moon.

The Education Committee of the Renfrewshire County Council, which had by now taken over responsibility from the Education Authority, had more down to earth business on their hands. They were responsible for the education of over 50,000 pupils in the county, and it is probable that most of the committee members were unaware that they had responsibility for the little school at Side, where by this time the roll had decreased to only 22 pupils. However, on the death of Mabel Maclaren, they would have been made aware of the existence of the school through the need to appoint a new teacher. Not surprisingly, they questioned the need for its continued existence. The facilities in the school, which still had no electricity, no gas, no running water and no flush toilets, not to mention the limited equipment and facilities for teaching, were well below the standards of the rest of the county. Roads and transport facilities were much improved, and the committee must have considered the possibility of closing the school and transporting the 22 children to the village school.

Before making their decision, they decided to take a plebiscite of the parents of the children then attending the school. In the meantime they appointed Mrs. Elizabeth Browning as teacher, making it clear to her that her appointment was temporary, and not offering her the tenancy of the school house.

There were ten parents with children at the school, and not surprisingly, they voted for continuation of the school, though one voted against. So the authority decided to continue to support the school, though on a temporary basis, and invited applications throughout the county for the post of temporary headmistress. As one might have expected there were no applications, for by now the school was beginning to look decidedly out of date, and the temporary nature of the appointment suggested that the successful candidate would not enjoy a long career there. So Mrs. Browning kept her job, and when she pointed out that the condition of the schoolhouse was deteriorating "through lack of firing", the Education Committee offered her the tenancy, and she and her family moved in.

It was important to the Browning family that Elizabeth secured the job of teacher at Side. Mr. Browning had started a picture framing business in Glasgow some years earlier, but the business failed as did many in the years of the Depression, and other employment would have been hard to find. Salaries of women teachers were modest in the early 1930's, starting at £130 per annum, but at least the schoolhouse was provided. The Brownings had a son, James, who had been going to school in Glasgow, and who now attended his mother's school at Side before transferring later to the Greenock High School.

There were some unconventional features of the Browning's lifestyle. Firstly, it was unusual for a married woman to work in the 1930's, and would probably have been out of the question 20 years earlier. Possibly the Education Committee accepted the situation simply because there were no other candidates who came forward. Secondly, her husband looked after the house and did the cooking, an accepted role arrangement nowadays, but unusual in 1930.

The following year the roll fell yet again, and the council decided to treat the school as an annexe of the village school. From this time, the Side school ceased to appear directly on any list of the council, and the

The Side School

whole question of its continuation gradually lost their attention, allowing the school to embark on its final quarter century of existence with little or no attention from the council. Mrs. Browning wrote in her log:

> *"The school from now becomes a "side" school of Kilmacolm"*

Part of the arrangement for the school was that after the age of eight, children would be transferred to the village school. Mr. Steele, head of the village school and now also in charge of Side, visited his annexe in September 1934 and discovered that there were eleven children in attendance out of a roll of twelve. He decided that four of them should transfer to the village school - and then there were seven!

Mrs. Browning quickly found her place in the community. She was both friendly and influential in the style of the old time dominies. Her son said that she "ruled the countryside". Every evening she got her milk from the farm at Margaret's Mill just up the road, stopping for a blather on the way. She never troubled to lock the door. In those days, people trusted one another, and no one felt that locking the door was necessary.

Elizabeth was a keen gardener. She often had the children weeding her garden, sometimes as a punishment for misbehaviour, or at times when there were too few miscreants to keep up with the needs of the garden, they did it anyway and were rewarded with a piece of chocolate cake and lemonade. In winter she had an equally practical punishment. Misbehaviour was rewarded by having to shovel snow from the paths round the school and schoolhouse buildings.

Mrs. Browning's teaching methods were dramatically different to those of her predecessors. With her small class of usually no more than a dozen children, there was no need for a regimented approach with children sitting in rows, with "eyes front and backs straight". She was able to maintain discipline with the children in informal groups round her table or sometimes sitting on the floor. She was a nature lover and spent a good deal of time with the children out of the classroom in the surrounding countryside, learning about the plants and wildlife. She knew of a fox's lair up the hill, and at times positioned the class downwind of the lair to watch the activities of the foxes. At the top of the Side Hill they could see the railway line between Kilmacolm and Port Glasgow, and some of the young children got their first sight of a steam train on one of these outings. On one occasion it was said that when she anticipated a visit from the school inspector, she took the class out of sight up the hill and taught them there until the inspector had grown tired of waiting and gone away.

The Inspectors managed to catch Mrs. Browning and her class in school in 1936 however, and the report of their visit read:

> *"All pupils beyond Junior division are now conveyed to Kilmacolm for further instruction. The junior and infant children who continue in attendance at this school are obviously happy in their work and show an engaging frankness under examination. General progress in the usual class subjects is distinctly creditable"*

In the 1930s the children got a number of extra holidays. The school was closed for a political meeting and then a General Election in 1931 when King George asked Ramsay MacDonald to form a National Coalition government in response to the problems of the Depression. In 1935 they got time off to celebrate the centenary of Walter Scott, the wedding of the Duke of Gloucester, and then the General Election that brought Stanley Baldwin to office as Prime Minister. In 1936 the school was closed for the funeral of George V, and after the turmoil of the abdication of Edward VIII, they got a holiday to celebrate the coronation of George VI.

In some Scottish towns at this time, two thirds of the work force was unemployed. The shipyards at Port Glasgow and Greenock were idle. During the week, some of the unemployed men left the towns and came to seek casual work on the farms, determined not to spend their time idling in the pubs and street corners. They did jobs like erecting barns, and slept in home made shelters, living off milk and potatoes supplied by the farmers in exchange for their labour. There is a curious memento from one of these workers, a man called John Roger, who carved a sundial in one of the smooth flat rocks just above the school where the children used to play. When Mrs. Browning took her class on nature study excursions up the hill, she demonstrated to the children how a sundial worked, using her walking stick held to the centre of the stone to create a shadow. The sundial can still be found a little way up the Side hill above the school.

In 1934 the Education Committee established a scale for the award of clothing and meals to the children of low-income parents. For example, a family with four children and an income of less than £1-19-7 (£1.98) got free boots, clothing and school meals. If the same family's income was more than £1-19-7 but less than £2-1-7 (£2.08) they just got the boots and clothing.

At about the same date, the Master of Works of the council submitted a report to the Education Committee on the cost of supplying all the schools in the county with toilet paper and the appropriate fittings. The cost estimate was not recorded, but whatever it was, the Education Committee decided that it was an unnecessary luxury in those difficult times and resolved that no action should be taken.

In 1939 the country was at war again. Mrs. Browning's son James went off to fight in Burma in the air force, and throughout the county male teachers left in great numbers to serve in His Majesty's Forces. A number of them returned some months later having been discharged from the armed forces on medical grounds, and an even smaller number was allowed to continue in their teaching jobs, having been registered as conscientious objectors. Even in this situation where they had a serious shortage of teaching staff, the Renfrewshire Education Committee were reluctant to consider employing married women as teachers.

It was not only teachers that were in short supply. Elsewhere in the county, school buildings were requisitioned for use by the military, and children had to be transported to alternative schools where space was available. There were also shortages of food, and children were enlisted in the "Dig For Victory" campaign, harvesting potatoes and grain just as they had in the Great War. Children and teachers helped in many schools to turn their sports fields over to growing vegetables. Raw materials for making paper were also scarce, and the schools collected up used exercise books, jotters and worn out text books for recycling. Coal was in short supply and the school managers transferred available supply from school to school to try to make ends meet.

Lessons in Geography were problematic because at the start of the war, head teachers had been instructed to gather up all of their maps and atlases and put them under lock and key, in case they fell into the hands of the enemy following an invasion. After a year without these materials the authorities agreed to let the maps be brought out again for teaching, but continued to make head teachers responsible for their safekeeping after lessons. Fear of an invasion was very real. At the Watt Memorial School in Greenock, teachers were instructed to confine their Wireless Telegraphy Classes to British subjects and the subjects of allied nations.

Temporary military buildings sprang up next to the school where an air observation post was set up supporting nearby searchlight and anti-aircraft gun emplacements. In the middle of the night, young soldiers nervously made their way up the hillside to their observation post at the top of the Side hill where in daytime the children played. The soldiers were young men, unused to the countryside and nervous, not because they anticipated enemy action, but because of the shadowy shapes of the cattle they kept coming up against in the dark.

In 1940 there was an unusually severe winter with heavy snow on the ground and the temperature was so low that the soldiers left their wooden huts and slept in the school, rekindling the fire that had kept the children warm during the day. The area was cut off for a time and milk was delivered by horse-drawn toboggan. At one time a Lysander aircraft parachuted in supplies.

Greenock experienced severe air raids in May 1941 when the Germans directed their bombs against the shipbuilding yards on the banks of the Clyde. A number of schools throughout the county were damaged. Children from the shipbuilding areas were evacuated to the safety of the countryside and a number of them went to the schools in Kilmacolm. In May 1941 the schools were closed when teachers were brought in to help assess war damage claims after the bombing. Afterwards teachers were issued with adhesive netting that they had to apply to the classroom windows and then coat with varnish as a protection against splintering glass caused by bombing.

The road alongside the school was busy with traffic at this time. In fine weather the boys would eat their lunch sitting astride the stone wall on the boundary of the school, watching out for heavy lorries making slow progress with oversize loads along the narrow road.

right: the Westside Annexe of the Kilmacolm Public School, 1951
back row, left to right: James Browning, Elizabeth Browning, Margaret Laird, Betty McTaggart, Hugh Black
the children, left to right: Sandy McIntyre, Hugh McIntyre, Elizabeth McDougal, Bill Kerr, John Kerr, Jimmy Black, Janet Crawford, Alastair McIntyre, Isobel Jackson, David Black, Alan Black

The Side School

The lorries carried ship components for the Clyde yards, having to use this road to avoid the low bridge at Bishopton on the direct route. After finishing their sandwiches, the children usually spent the rest of their lunch break up the hill. When Mrs. Browning appeared, calling "School!" to start the afternoon session, this was the signal for the children to vanish out of sight among the bracken.

By the time the war ended in 1945, there were only six pupils left at Side and the School Management Committee recommended that the school be closed, but for some reason the recommendation was not adopted by the County Education Committee. Six years later Mrs. Browning advised the Committee that she was due to retire in April of that year, offering to carry on teaching until the end of the school year. Once more, the existence of the school was brought to the notice of the Education Committee, and the question of its continued existence came up again. This time there was no reprieve, and the Committee decided to close the school down at the end of the session, transferring the eleven remaining children from Side to the village school.

The future of the school building was placed in the hands of the Properties Subcommittee. The Chairman and Vice Chairman of the committee took a trip into the country to see this out of the way school for themselves, and to decide what to do with the building. They reported back that they knew of *"no educational purpose to which the school could be put"*, and decided to dispose of the building. Luckily none of the School Management Committee who had struggled to build the school a century earlier was around to hear this ignominious assessment of the school.

Epilogue

The Education Committee were thoughtful enough to give reasonable notice of termination of tenancy to Mrs. Browning who continued to live alone in the school house, her husband having died some time previously. After a few months she moved to Gourock where, unlike her predecessors, she enjoyed a long retirement.

At the back of the log book, the head teacher of the village school recorded the final demise of the school:

"Mrs. Browning discontinued entries in this log book in view of the changed status at Westside noted under date 3/9/34. She continued as teacher at Westside till the end of session 1950 - 1951 having been granted an extension beyond the usual retiral age in April of 1951. In September 1951 the pupils were transferred to Kilmacolm. Mrs. Browning removed from the schoolhouse (to Gourock) early in December 1951 and the property was then disposed of by auction"

The school building fetched a very modest price at auction. It became a private dwelling house and in time the school room was incorporated to become part of the house, but not before being used at one time for keeping chickens. Although a number of modifications have been made over the years, including the provision of mains water and electricity, the external appearance of the building is little changed from that of the original Victorian building, the substantial walls of up to three feet in thickness not lending themselves to easy modification.

It is not unusual for people to look back on their early school days as a pleasurable experience, though sometimes with a vision coloured by the passage of time, but with the men and women who were pupils at Side in the last few decades of its existence, there seems to be a particularly strong consensus that they really did enjoy their school days there. When the children transferred to the village school at the age of nine or ten they were said to be typically a year in advance of the pupils already there. The small class size and the enlightened teaching methods of Mrs. Browning were obviously effective.

The school had changed beyond recognition since the children had first crowded round the open fire to read from the bible in the primitive building erected some six generations earlier. The idea of holding nature study classes up the slopes of the hill would have been unthinkable at the early school.

There is no doubt that the school served a useful purpose in those early days when travelling to the village school was out of the question. Whether it outlived its usefulness in later years is open to question, and the School Board back in 1875 might well have decided that it would have been better to transport the children to the village school where facilities were always superior. Nevertheless they did take on Side, and we can be thankful for the survival of this little community school which with all its idiosyncrasies, poor sanitation and limited facilities managed to achieve in its time a standard of excellence that surpassed its larger neighbours.

It seems appropriate to let Nigel MacMillan have the last word. The closing paragraph from his reminiscences seems particularly appropriate:

> *"I am afraid that I have taxed your patience with those old-world stories. Whether they were worth writing I cannot judge. They flash across the*

conscious sense now and then like streamers flitting across a cloudless sky on a dark night. Looking back 60 or 70 years I feel that man has been making great progress. Even in the space of an ordinary life, man has swept forward by leaps and bounds. No other period in the world's history can compare with the past 50 years. But great as our progress has been, we feel that we are on the threshold of still greater achievements. Experience is teacher in nature's school whose curriculum is without bounds or limits"

Bibliography

Kilmacolm, a Parish History	Rev James Murray MA
A Kirk Without a Steeple	Elizabeth M Main
Scottish Voices	T C Smout and Sydney Wood
A Century of Scottish People	T C Smout
People and Society in Scotland: An Exploration into Scottish Education	H Corr
Manual of the Education Acts for Scotland	A C Sellars
History of Scottish Education	J Scotland
The Statistical Account of Scotland, 1799	
The New Statistical Account of Scotland, 1845	
The Third Statistical Account of Scotland, 1959	
Ordnance Gazetteer of Scotland, 1884	

Archives

Kilmacolm Westside School Log books	Glasgow City Archives
Minute Books of the School Board of the Parish of Kilmacolm	Glasgow City Archives
Renfrewshire Education Authority: Minutes of Meetings of Authority and Committee	Paisley Reference Library
Kilmacolm Heritors Minute Book	Scottish Record Office, Edinburgh
Jordanhill College of Education: Teacher Training Records	Jordanhill, Glasgow
Old Parish Records of Renfrewshire	Paisley Museum
Renfrewshire Census Records	Paisley Museum

The Teachers

c.1816 -1819	**Robert Muir**	Married with 2 children. Transferred to Glenmill school in c.1819
c.1836 -1864	**Daniel Ferguson**	b. 1797. Single
c.1870 -1873	**Rob Robertson**	b. 1846. Single.
1873 - 1877	**William Campbell**	b. 1844. Single. Salary £75 in 1876 rising to £85 in 1877. Resigned in 1877 to go to the Public School of Swiney, Lybster
1875 - 1878	Lillias Laird	Sewing mistress.
1877 - 1884	**Stewart Archibald**	b. 1845. Married with 3 children. Salary £75 in 1877 rising to £85 in 1880. Services terminated by the School Board in 1884.
1878 - 1884	Mary Archibald	Sewing mistress.
1884 - 1905	**Annie Craig Bell**	b. 1852. Single. Salary £50 in 1884 rising to £65 in 1901. Retired due to ill health in May 1905. Died March 1906 after 20 years service.
1905 - 1930	**Mabel Elizabeth Maclaren**	b. 1880. Single. Salary £75 in 1912 rising to £25 in 1918. Died during the school holidays in 1930 after 25 years service.
1907	Sarah Wylie	Assistant teacher.
1907 - 1913	Sarah Farrell	Assistant teacher.
1913 - 1915	Ann D MacKinlay	Assistant teacher.
1916 - 1917	Flora MacKinnon	Assistant teacher.
1917 - 1925	Elizabeth L Lang	Assistant teacher. A former pupil of the Side school. Transferred to the village school in 1925 because of the fall in roll at Side.
1930 - 1951	**Elizabeth J Browning**	Retired in July 1951 after 21 years service.

Westside Subscription School Management Committee

1873
Rev James Eckford Fyfe (chairman)	UP Minister
Alexander Graham Duncan McDougal	farmer, Dippany
James Baxter	farmer, High Craiglinscheoch
Donald Black	farmer, Auchenfoil
John Scott	
John Chalmers	

Kilmacolm School Board Members

1873 to 1875
Sir Michael Robert Shaw-Stewart *(chairman)*	Lord Lieutenant of Renfrewshire
resigned and was replaced by:	
Horatio Renaud Babington Peile	Factor, Inverkip House, Inverkip
Frederick George Daniel Bryan	Factor
Robert Lindsay	Bookseller
Thomas Smith Thoms	Farmer, Auchenbothie
George Wood	Merchant, Thornwood, Kilmacolm

1876 to 1878
Horatio Peile *(chairman)*	Factor, Inverkip House, Inverkip
John Thomson	Farmer, North Dennistoun
Thomas Smith Thoms	Farmer, Auchenbothie
George Wood: *died in office and was replaced by:*	Merchant, Thornwood, Kilmacolm
Robert Lindsay	Bookseller
Archibald Connal Stevenson	Glass manufacturer, Mansfield, Kilmacolm

The Side School

1879 to 1881 Horatio Peile *(chairman)*   Factor, Inverkip House, Inverkip
　　　　　　　　Alexander Bartlemore   Banker in Johnston, Thornwood, Kilmacolm
　　　　　　　　Thomas Smith Thoms   Farmer, Auchenbothie
　　　　　　　　Rev James Murray   Parish minister, the Manse, Kilmacolm
　　　　　　　　Rev James Eckford Fyfe   UP minister, Kilmacolm

1882 to 1884 Horatio Peile *(chairman)*   Factor, Inverkip House, Inverkip
　　　　　　　　Alexander Laird   Merchant, Meadowside, Kilmacolm
　　　　　　　　Thomas Smith Thoms   Farmer, Auchenbothie
　　　　　　　　William McKee   Merchant, Marketplace, Kilmacolm
　　　　　　　　Alexander Bartlemore   Banker in Johnston, Thornwood, Kilmacolm
　　　　　　　　Rev James Murray   Parish minister, the Manse, Kilmacolm
　　　　　　　　Andrew Mitchell   Linen merchant, South Park, Kilmacolm

1885 to 1887 Rev James Murray *(chairman)*   Parish minister, the Manse, Kilmacolm
　　　　　　　　Horatio Peile   Factor, Inverkip House, Inverkip
　　　　　　　　Alexander Laird   Merchant, Meadowside, Kilmacolm
　　　　　　　　William McKee   Merchant, Marketplace, Kilmacolm
　　　　　　　　Neil Robson   Iron Master, Grafton, Kilmacolm
　　　　　　　　John Thompson   Farmer, Dennistoun
　　　　　　　　Andrew Mitchell   Linen merchant, South Park, Kilmacolm

1888 to 1890 Horatio Peile *(chairman)*   Factor, Inverkip House, Inverkip
  Rev James Murray   Parish minister, the Manse, Kilmacolm
  Alexander Laird   Merchant, Meadowside, Kilmacolm
  Neil Robson   Iron Master, Grafton, Kilmacolm
  Peter Woodrow   Builder, Marketplace, Kilmacolm
  Andrew Mitchell   Warehouseman, South Park, Kilmacolm
  Rev James Eckford Fyfe   UP Minister, Kilmacolm

1891 to 1893 Horatio Peile *(chairman)*   Factor, Inverkip House, Inverkip
  Rev James Murray   Parish minister, the Manse, Kilmacolm
  George Robertson   Silk Throwster, Moorecote, Kilmacolm
  Peter Woodrow   Architect, Marketplace, Kilmacolm
  Rev James Gregory   Minister, Kilmacolm
  Rev James Eckford Fyfe   UP Minister, Kilmacolm
  John Kinlock   Hardware merchant, Ellenbank, Kilmacolm

1894 to 1896 Horatio Peile *(chairman)*   Factor, Inverkip House, Inverkip
  Rev James Murray   Parish minister, the Manse, Kilmacolm
  William Gibb-Stewart   Painter, Mossgiel, Kilmacolm
  Peter Woodrow   Architect, Marketplace, Kilmacolm
  Rev James Gregory   Minister, Kilmacolm
  Rev James Eckford Fyfe   UP Minister, Kilmacolm
  Donald McLean Main   Commercial Traveller, Lyle buildings

The Side School

1897 to 1899   Horatio Peile *(chairman)*   Factor, Inverkip House, Inverkip
Rev James Murray — Parish minister, the Manse, Kilmacolm
William Gibb-Stewart — Painter, Mossgiel, Kilmacolm
Peter Woodrow — Architect, Marketplace, Kilmacolm
John Binnie — Stockbroker, Launceton, Kilmacolm
Rev James Eckford Fyfe — UP Minister, Kilmacolm
    died in office and was replaced by
Rev Thomas Gregory — FC Minister, Cargen Lodge, Kilmacolm
Donald McLean Main — Commercial Traveller, Lyle buildings

1900 to 1902   Horatio Peile *(chairman)* — Factor, Inverkip House, Inverkip
Rev James Murray — Parish minister, the Manse, Kilmacolm
Archibald Duncan Ferguson — Writer, Lydden, Kilmacolm
Frederick Lewis Maitland Moir — Secretary, Mandela, Kilmacolm
Robert A Bryden — Architect, 15 Dalhouse Street, Glasgow
Rev Thomas Gregory — FC Minister, Cargen Lodge, Kilmacolm
Donald McLean Main — Commercial Traveller, Lyle buildings

1903 to 1905   Horatio Peile *(chairman)* — Factor, Inverkip House, Inverkip
Archibald Duncan Ferguson — Writer, Lydden, Kilmacolm
Frederick Lewis Maitland Moir — Secretary, Mandela, Kilmacolm
Robert A Bryden — Architect, 15 Dalhouse Street, Glasgow
Rev Thomas Gregory — FC Minister, Cargen Lodge, Kilmacolm
Donald McLean Main — Commercial Traveller, Lyle buildings
Archibald Campbell

1906 to 1908	Horatio Peile *(chairman)*	Factor, Inverkip House, Inverkip
	Archibald Duncan Ferguson	Writer, Lydden, Kilmacolm
	Isobel Reid Barr	Eredine, Kilmacolm
	Peter Alexander Laird	Surgeon, Derena, Kilmacolm
	Bennet McLean	Chemist, Englewood, Kilmacolm
	Rev Thomas Gregory	FC Minister, Cargen Lodge, Kilmacolm
	David Andrew Steven	Joiner, Wardend, KIlmacolm
1909 to 1913	Horatio Peile *(chairman)*	Factor, Inverkip House, Inverkip
	Rev James Murray	Parish Minister, the Manse, Kilmacolm
	Isobel Reid Barr	Eredine, Kilmacolm
	William Baird Bain	Engineer, Strathearn, Kilmacolm
	Bennet McLean	Chemist, Englewood, Kilmacolm
	Rev Thomas Gregory	FC Minister, Cargen Lodge, Kilmacolm
	George Maitland	Leather merchant, Dunerag, Kilmacolm
1914 to 1918	Horatio Peile *(chairman)*	Factor, Inverkip House, Inverkip
	Rev James Murray	Parish Minister, the Manse, Kilmacolm
	Robert Colville Conway	Cabinet maker, The Firs, Kilmacolm
	William Baird Bain	Engineer, Strathearn, Kilmacolm
	Bennet McLean	Chemist, Englewood, Kilmacolm
	Harry Watson	Clothier, Stewart Place, Kilmacolm
	George Maitland	Leather merchant, Dunerag, Kilmacolm